the long italian lunch

Julie Biuso

the long
italian lunch

Julie Biuso

recipe photographs by Ian Batchelor

over 70 dishes that are too good to hurry

NEW HOLLAND

DEDICATION

In memory of Mamma Rosa, and to Margot, Marcella and Isanna, with much gratitude.

Published in 2003 by
New Holland Publishers (UK) Ltd
London • Cape Town • Sydney • Auckland

Garfield House
86–88 Edgware Road
London
W2 2EA
United Kingdom
www.newhollandpublishers.com

80 McKenzie Street
Cape Town 8001
South Africa

Level 1, Unit 4, 14 Aquatic Drive
Frenchs Forest, NSW 2086
Australia

218 Lake Road
Northcote, Auckland
New Zealand

ISBN 1 84330 383 3

Senior Editor: Clare Hubbard
Designer: Ian Sandom
Production: Hazel Kirkman
Recipe photography: Ian Batchelor
Location photography: Eugenio Biuso
Editorial Direction: Rosemary Wilkinson

1 3 5 7 9 10 8 6 4 2

Reproduction by Colourscan Overseas Co PTE Ltd, Singapore
Printed and bound by Times Offset (M) Sdn Bhd, Malaysia

NOTE

In the recipes use either metric or imperial measurements, never a combination of the two, as exact conversions are not always possible.

ACKNOWLEDGEMENTS

This book is all about my closest friends and family, the fabulous food we've shared, and a lot of luck. First, a special thanks to my husband Remo and our hungrier-than-ever children Luca and Ilaria for their unwavering support. Ray Richards, my literary agent and friend for 19 years, has been instrumental in making this book a reality. Thanks for everything Ray.

The big thanks goes to New Holland (UK) for taking me seriously and producing this book and New Holland (New Zealand) for their nurturing and support – Belinda Cooke, John Beaufoy, Elena Mannion, Yvonne McFarlane, Rosemary Wilkinson, Clare Hubbard, Yvonne Thynne and Terry Shaughnessy – it's been a pleasure to work with you all.

The stunningly gorgeous lip-smacking food images taken by Ian Batchelor speak volumes. I knew they were good shots when we took them, but seeing them in print makes my heart go pitter-patter and I want to eat the food all over again!

Another very special thank-you goes to my nephew, Eugenio Biuso, who took the location and ingredients shots. You're a treasure!

Special thanks to Lufthansa German Airlines, New Zealand, for their assistance in travel to Europe.

Contents

Foreword

It seems to me that Julie's dream is to invite to lunch an enormous number of people, and to cook for them. She would serve at this banquet the dishes she loves, so that her guests can love them too. She would talk to each of them, to find out if what they are eating is delighting them in the same way it delighted her to prepare it.

This book is for her the closest thing to her dream. Julie cannot invite every one of you to lunch, but the splendid dishes that she would cook for you are offered on these pages. Read and try to recreate them. You are her guests.

CARLO PETRINI,
PRESIDENT OF SLOW FOOD MOVEMENT

Introduction

I love long Italian lunches – I was smitten from the first time I sat around a crowded table jostling elbows, passing platters of food with laughing, cajoling, arguing Italians!

Italian lunches are leisurely, especially at feast-time, and I've never wanted them to end. It's as if some magic is created when friends and family gather to share in the ritual of nourishing body and soul. It's a time to be treasured and a time to celebrate the cook who has filled the house with tempting smells and laid on the table food which tempts and titillates, sustains and satisfies.

The frenzied pace with which most of us now conduct our lives is making inroads into this enjoyment of food and into the fabric of family life. Fast food is getting faster – it has to be ready NOW. Advertisers are constantly telling people, "No one wants to spend long in the kitchen these days," (so buy our convenience product!). Nothing makes me madder. People are being scared out of the kitchen and are made to feel guilty about time spent lovingly preparing food. Soon our young won't know how to cook – only how to reheat and serve ready-made food.

Well, I want to make a stand. I'm all for the family, warts and all, coming together at meal-times, gathering around the table, eating together, discussing the day, sharing ideas, debating and arguing light-heartedly. Not that I am averse to good planning and sensible shortcuts and I definitely favour fresh food which is quick to put together. But I want, just occasionally, for people to slow down, spend a bit of time in the kitchen making something delicious, something which will bring joy to family and friends and enrich their lives. That's what is inside my heart. I've always loved cooking because it's a way of giving pleasure to people, while strengthening bonds with family and friends.

Enjoy then, the time it takes to make and eat these Long Italian Lunches.

Julie Biuso

Preface

Like many others, I avidly read Elizabeth David's passionate accounts of travelling through Italy, but it wasn't until I set foot on Italian soil in 1975 and experienced Italy for myself that I truly understood what she meant.

Instead of trying to imagine the smells and tastes, I began living them. My heart fluttered with excitement at every bite, at every sniff and whiff, every sip and sup. I drank Italy in, in big gulps. Every day was a journey of discovery. The markets, the way the people chose produce, the attention they gave to ripeness and freshness, the wonderful smells wafting in the streets every day around lunchtime – it was all a visual and odoriferous awakening. It was hard not to be seduced and I didn't resist, I couldn't resist, I just surrendered with an open mouth and tried every-thing offered to me, searching out new food at every opportunity.

I was lucky to be welcomed into an Italian family of good cooks and many of the recipes in this book are dishes direct from my late mother-in-law, Mamma Rosa's, kitchen or from her daughters, Margot and Marcella and her daughter-in-law Isanna. Mamma Rosa was a great cook, there's no doubt about it. The kitchen, even in summer when it was as hot as a furnace, was a magnet and everyone made their way there several times during the morning to lift lids on pots, sniff, stir and comment. Everyone had an opinion about food. Everyone talked about food, all day and all night!

This was all part of my Italian education, which formed a palette of smells, colours, tastes and textures in my senses. Over time I have learnt that there is no such thing as "Italian cuisine". It remains regional, in spite of globalization. The rich foods of Emilia-Romagna, where butter and cream are used lavishly and fresh pasta is favoured over dried, are vastly different to the earthy simplicity of Tuscan cooking, which features grills, roasts and vegetables, flavoured with little more than a dusting of salt and a dousing of extra virgin olive oil. Yet these two regions share a border many kilometres long.

The defining characteristic of the food of Italy is the clarity of flavour and texture, whether it is a bracing sauce that stimulates the tastebuds or a sauce of such softness and subtlety that your palate feels as if it is cushioned in velvet. Every ingredient is used for a reason, forming an integral part of the dish. This flavour potency forms the backbone of the cuisine, giving it vibrancy and an assertive character. Fearless cooking! Cooking for flavour, texture, taste and nourishment, for satisfaction, satiation and dare I say it, greed!

"Keep it simple" is the essence of Italian cooking. The other points are obvious: fresh, seasonal food, don't skimp on the oil, season food generously with salt and taste as you go along. Be generous in the best Italian spirit. Put on some of your favourite music, whack up the volume, invite friends and family over, get into the kitchen and cook up a storm. You'll be loved for it!

Ingredients

Italian cooking and the ingredients that are used in it are now familiar the world over. Supermarket shelves are laden with the meats, cheeses, vegetables, herbs, oils, pasta and rice that we need to make wonderful Italian dishes. Over the next few pages I'm going to pass on to you some of the tips and hints that I've picked up over the years from my family. You should also refer to the detailed glossary (see pages 125–127) which gives information on the key ingredients used in this book.

Artichokes

PREPARATION Always use a stainless steel knife (not a carbon one) to cut artichokes; carbon taints them, causing blackening to the artichoke and the knife (if you accidentally use a carbon steel knife, clean it after with half a lemon; it will remove the black and the nasty metallic smell).

There are several ways to prepare an artichoke, depending on how you want to use it. First, fill a bowl with water and squeeze the juice of a lemon into it. As the artichokes are prepared, put them in the water; the lemon will help prevent them discolouring. It's a good idea to wear thin food preparation gloves when preparing artichokes to prevent them staining the hands.

Cut off the top third of the artichoke and discard (the tips of the leaves). Trim the stalk; if it is very fibrous, peel the outside of it. The artichoke can be boiled as it is and the choke removed after cooking; this is suitable when artichokes are to be served cold. If you want to cook the artichoke with seasoning or stuffing, spread the leaves apart, opening and loosening the trimmed artichoke. Remove the mauve-coloured leaves in the centre, then press the soft, yellowish leaves away from the centre until a

cavity is formed and the choke is revealed. The choke is a collection of fibrous hairs, which should be totally scraped out as it's inedible, even after cooking. Use a pointed teaspoon to remove it, but take care to remove only the hairy fibre, because directly below this is the meaty base of the artichoke (referred to as the fond or heart). The artichoke is then ready for seasoning or stuffing.

When the artichokes are to be sliced, it is easier to cut off the tips, slice the artichoke in half, extract the half-choke and then slice thinly.

Aubergine

PREPARATION Most aubergine recipes recommend that you sprinkle the sliced or chopped aubergine with salt before cooking to draw out bitter juices. It's worth doing if the aubergine is bitter, but a waste of time if it is not. The question is, how do you tell if an aubergine is bitter?

In my experience, immature aubergines which are heavy for their size, and those tinged with a fair amount of green underneath the skin (visible when you cut or slice them) will be bitter. There is sometimes a detectable smell of unripeness or greenness too, similar to the smell you get when you cut open a heavy, firm green pepper. Also, aubergines which are full of seeds have a tendency to be bitter. If you've ever eaten a bitter aubergine, you'll know how unpleasant it is. If in doubt, salting is a wise precaution. However, moisture, which is a result of salting, is the enemy of hot oil – it causes spitting and lowers the overall temperature of the oil – and aubergines fry better if they haven't been salted. Salt is the aubergine's catch-22.

COOKING So, how much oil do you use when frying aubergines? The tip is: the hotter the oil, the less of it the aubergines will absorb. Try for yourself. Put a few slices of aubergine into a moderately hot pan over a medium heat with three tablespoons of oil and watch the aubergine suck up the oil like a thirsty sponge. But fry the slices in "boiling oil", as the Italians do, and you'll be astounded by the difference.

I credit the Sicilians for teaching me how to cook aubergines. The aubergines are not salted before they are cooked. They are sliced, air-dried briefly, then lowered into oil that's so hot it's shimmering and on the point of smoking. They emerge a burnished golden brown with crisp, taut skin and creamy interior. The thing you mustn't fear is the temperature of the oil – there has to be a good quantity of it and it has to be hot.

Another successful method, particularly useful when the aubergine is to be incorporated into a pie or layered dish, is to oven-bake them (see page 115).

Peppers

ROASTING If you have barbecuing facilities, the peppers can be roasted on the barbecue grill-rack and will take on a wonderfully smoky flavour. Alternatively, put the peppers on a rack in an oven preheated to 200°C/400°F/gas 6 and cook, turning occasionally with tongs, for about 20 minutes, or until they are blistered and charred. (They will be softer prepared this way.) Transfer to a board and, when cool, peel off the skins and slip out the cores and seeds. Putting a sheet of aluminium foil underneath the peppers to catch the drips will save messing up the oven. My favourite way is to roast them over a gas flame because they char quickly, taking on a wonderful flavour, but retain a good texture. Put two or three peppers in the gas flame on a hob. Cook until charred all over, turning with tongs. Cool, then peel. Some recipes call for the pepper juices to be saved for use in the recipe.

The roasted peppers can be used immediately or kept for several days, covered and refrigerated. They are delicious on their own, drizzled with extra virgin olive oil, flecked with herbs or dotted with capers, olives, anchovy pieces etc. Serve as a nibble or on top of pizzas and crostini.

Tomatoes

FRESH VERSUS TINNED There is no point in making a tomato sauce with hot-house grown or unripe tomatoes because it will be a let-down – either pale and watery, insipid, acidic or all of these. Use tomatoes ripened on the vine, grown in a sunny climate, which have a fresh fruit flavour. Choose a fleshier type: what you need for a good sauce is pulp, not water.

If good, fresh tomatoes are not available, use Italian canned tomatoes, preferably the San Marzanno variety.

PRE-SIEVED ITALIAN TOMATOES Sold under various names such as "Passata", this product makes a quick tomato sauce even faster. The advantage is not only a quicker sauce, but a sweeter one, as the seeds have been removed (tomato seeds, especially if crushed, are bitter). Cook pre-sieved tomatoes in oil with a few seasonings and, in less than 15 minutes, a rich red sauce is yours.

Mushrooms

STORING Mushrooms stored in plastic (at room temperature or in the fridge) quickly sweat or become moist, then turn soggy and rot. Store them either in an unsealed paper bag or unsealed in a large plastic bag or container lined with absorbent kitchen paper.

PREPARATION Reconstitute porcini (or cèpes) by soaking for 30 minutes in warm water. Put the porcini in a sieve and rinse under running water. Tip them into a bowl and pour on the specified amount of hot water. Leave to soak for 30 minutes, then lift them out of the liquid using a slotted spoon and transfer to a sieve (reserve the soaking liquid). Rinse well under running water then chop finely, discarding any woody bits. Strain the soaking liquid into a bowl through a sieve lined with a piece of absorbent paper. Strain again and use as required.

Garlic

TO CHOP OR CRUSH Garlic is traditionally chopped, not crushed. If you're cautious about this, just remember that Italians were cooking with garlic long before garlic crushers were invented. In most recipes the difference is hard to detect, but when it is, as in Isanna's free range eggs on page 19, where the pungent zing of chopped raw garlic is an integral part of the dish and the element which stops the egg yolks and oil becoming too rich, I suggest you prepare it this way. Chopped garlic is probably stronger because you use more of it and the pieces are bigger when they hit your palate. If you want a milder taste, use crushed garlic and less of it.

RAW GARLIC Under no circumstances should you use the last of the season's garlic raw in a dish –

if the garlic has started to sprout (small pale green sprout in the centre of the clove) it will repeat on you after eating it. Garlic crushers usually catch the sprout but if you want to remove it by hand, cut the clove in half and pick it out.

Chillies

"BIRD'S EYE" CHILLIES These minuscule dried hot chilli peppers are the nearest equivalent to the tongue-hot, small dried chillies (not to be confused with lip-burning or throat-burning varieties) used in various ways in Italy. These chillies can transform a very simple dish into one of notable character. Use them whole and discard before serving for a mild flavour, or crush or chop finely for a hotter, more powerful impact. They are an optional ingredient in many recipes in this book. If you don't like chillies simply leave them out.

Pesto

SERVING SECRETS If you have ever eaten a bowl of pasta dressed with an oil-based sauce such as pesto, which starts out tasting delicious, but half-way through it goes sort of heavy and oily, and the more cheese you put on the tackier and less appetizing it becomes, read on.

First, don't over-drain the pasta; leave a fair amount of moisture clinging to it. If you over-drain it the heat dries the surface of the pasta and the sauce sinks in instead of sliding over and coating the pasta.

Toss the drained pasta with a little butter to flavour it and to help the sauce flow over. Dilute the pesto – not with more oil, which would throw out the balance of flavours and make the pesto too oily on the palate – but with a little of the hot pasta water (it brings up the colour too). Toss pesto and pasta and add enough hot pasta water (1–3 tablespoons) to enable the pesto to flow easily over the pasta. You may shake your head in disbelief at the idea of adding hot pasta water, but the result is delicious beyond description.

Salads

A salad spinner is an excellent method for drying washed salad greens and herbs, causing little damage. The old Italian trick of bundling the salad items in a clean cloth and shaking it vigorously out the window is quaint, but bruises the leaves beyond repair.

Once the leaves are dried they can be kept crisp by transferring them to a plastic bag and chilling them in the fridge for an hour or several hours, but it is best not to tear the leaves into bite-size pieces until assembling the salad because the leaves can discolour and nutrients are lost.

Pasta

There are two main types of pasta: fresh and dried. One is not better than the other. They are different in their construction, in the way they are cooked and in the sauces which best suit them. Fresh pasta is more tender and delicate, absorbs sauce more readily and is better suited to lighter, delicate sauces, particularly those made with butter and/or cream.

Italian dried pasta is without exception a superior product to that made elsewhere. It bulks up well during cooking, doesn't collapse once cooked, has a good creamy, wheaty taste and plenty of chew to it.

There are hundreds of pasta shapes. Historically, the shapes are a reflection of customs, regional influences, inventiveness, and provide a break from tedium, because pasta has been the staple food of Italy for hundreds of years and new ideas are always welcome, all stirred together with a little romance, a little humour and a lot of family love. Basically pasta can be divided into five types: long pasta (which includes spaghetti and noodles such as fettuccine); tubes (which include penne and rigatoni); special shapes (fusilli, conchiglie); stuffed pastas (tortelloni, cannelloni); and pasta shapes specifically designed for soups (orzi, stelline, alfabetini).

Long shapes, like spaghetti, taste best with olive oil-based sauces and sauces without big pieces of ingredients, although small clams and tiny mussels are used in some of the classic match-ups, such as *spaghetti alle vongole* (spaghetti with clams). What you need to think of here is whether all the sauce components can be twirled together on a fork with the spaghetti – if so, you're in business. If bits fall off the fork (not drips of sauce, but lumpy bits) you might be better serving the sauce with tube pasta next time or a wider noodle.

Noodles such as tagliatelle and fettuccine, (which is narrower than tagliatelle), when made with egg pasta, are often teamed with butter and cream-based sauces which cling to the rougher texture of the pasta. A classic matching is tagliatelle with Bolognese sauce.

Tubes are useful for catching lumpy bits of ingredients and sauce inside the hollows. They are quite bouncy to eat, providing lots of chew, and can take a textured sauce. Some shapes are served with cream-based sauces, such as garganelli, which is traditionally made by hand.

Mussels

PREPARATION Scrub them under running water with a stiff brush, then pull off the beards. Put the mussels in a large bowl and fill with cold water. Stir them around, then lift out into a clean bowl. Repeat the process until the water is clear and grit-free. Leave the mussels to soak for 15 minutes in fresh water. You should discard any mussels that open during cleaning and any that don't open after cooking.

Scaloppine

PREPARATION *Scaloppine* is the Italian name for thin slices of veal cut from a single muscle off the top of the animal's leg (called the "top round"). The meat must be cut across the grain or it will shrivel up on cooking and be tough to eat. The slices of veal need to be lightly flattened with a meat mallet to make them uniformly thin. Do not bash the meat, as it easily tears and turns to shreds. Cover the meat with a clean plastic bag or waxed paper and apply gentle pressure with the mallet, sliding it along the surface of the meat as you do so. This stretches the meat without damaging the tissues.

Menus

Good menu planning is about balancing different flavours, choosing dishes that work well together and, of course, using ingredients that are in season.

SPRING DINNER
SERVES 6

Fried asparagus p. 20
Need to increase the amount of ingredients to: 3 eggs; 750g (1lb 10oz) asparagus; 40g (1½oz) breadcrumbs; 4½ tbsp parmesan.

Veal fillet with green olives and fresh bay leaves p. 76
Roasted fennel p. 98
Salad of green leaves (your choice).

Lemon ricotta flan p. 102

Lemon ricotta flan

SUMMER MEAL
SERVES 6

Crab and lemon pasta p. 32
Need to increase the amount of ingredients to: 375g (13oz) pasta; 450ml (³/₄ pt) single cream; zest of 3 lemons; 1½ tbsp green peppercorns; 375g (13oz) crab meat; 3 tbsp parsley.

Poussins with crunchy prosciutto and sage butter p. 74
Fennel, sweet tomato and olive salad p. 97

Peaches stuffed with amaretti p. 104

ANTIPASTI LUNCH
SERVES 6–10

Isanna's free range eggs p. 19
Mozzarella and roasted red pepper salad p. 24
Flaky spinach pie p. 65
Bruschetta with tomato and orange p. 25

Serve the above with plenty of crusty bread, sliced salami, prosciutto or other cured meats, olives and chargrilled or wood-roasted bottled artichokes.

THE BIG LUNCH
SERVES 8

Steamed mussels with basil dressing p. 22
Cook extra mussels.

Venetian fish p. 68

Jumping spaghetti p. 34
Make double the quantity and toss it in two pans; or
Fettuccine with Roman style meat sauce p. 37
Increase pasta quantity to 750g (1lb 10oz) and make the sauce with 800g (1¾lb) canned tomatoes and 1.25kg (2½ lb) minced beef).

Roasted eye fillet wrapped in pancetta p. 80
Potatoes with rosemary p. 92
Salad of crisp green leaves (your choice).

Pine nut torte p. 107 or
Hazelnut and amaretti cupola p. 110
You could be naughty and serve both!

Jumping spaghetti

WINTER DINNER
SERVES 6

Parmesan with rocket leaves p. 25
Use a little extra rocket and parmesan.

Lamb abruzzi p. 81
Crunchy potato sticks p. 90
Withered carrots p. 96

Crumbly almond cake p. 105
Serve with Vin Santo.

WEEKDAY MEALS

Start with a platter of crunchy vegetables; choose from fennel bulbs, young carrots, red and yellow peppers, cucumber, small radishes and celery. Accompany with a dip of the best extra virgin olive oil you can afford. Have sea salt and a pepper grinder on the side and crusty bread, too. A selection of four vegetables and 120ml (4fl oz) of oil will be sufficient for four people.

Choose one of the following main courses and serve it with a salad of your choice:
Baked rigatoni with ricotta p. 45
Tart's spaghetti p. 36
Oven-baked aubergine p. 56 or mushroom risotto p. 58
Sausage coil with hot polenta and sautéed mushrooms p. 84
Leg of lamb with parmesan crust and crunchy potatoes p. 82

Finish the meal with a selection of fresh fruit.

Soups and Starters

Parmesan wafers

Wafer di parmigiano

Coarsely grated parmesan cheese can be baked until it melts, then shaped and filled with tasty morsels. Try it with one of the following – a small cube of fresh juicy pear, a scoop of pepper or quince jelly or a small curl of prosciutto.

250g (9oz) parmesan cheese

SERVES UP TO 10 AS NIBBLES

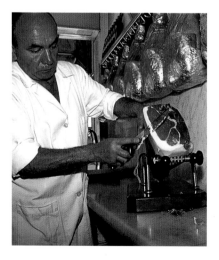

Preheat the oven to 210°C/410°F/gas 6. Grate the cheese coarsely. Put small mounds of cheese on a baking tray (cook six at a time) lined with a teflon baking sheet or baking parchment and cook for 4–5 minutes or until the cheese has melted and is lightly golden; don't overcook.

Leave the cheese wafers to settle for 30–40 seconds, then lift them off with a knife, curling them over as you do so. They will go their own way to some extent, forming interesting shapes, but the idea is to make a shape into which you can put a filling.

Cool the wafers on a rack, then store them in an airtight container until required (they can be made several hours in advance but are best eaten the day they are made).

Isanna's free range eggs

Uova di Isanna

This dish from my sister-in-law's kitchen requires few special ingredients and takes no more than 5 minutes to make, but it tastes sensational. Make it with the first of the season's mild garlic and eggs about four days old – it is difficult to peel very fresh, lightly-cooked eggs.

6 free-range medium eggs, at room
   temperature
salt
2 tbsp coarsely chopped parsley
1 tbsp finely chopped fresh garlic
freshly ground black pepper to taste
paprika
small black Ligurian "olivelle" olives
   (optional)
estate-bottled extra virgin olive oil

SERVES 4–6

To prevent the egg shells from cracking during cooking, use the point of a dressmaking pin to prick the rounded end of each egg. Carefully lower them into a pan of gently boiling water and cook for 7 minutes. Drain off the water, then let the cold tap run over the eggs for 5 minutes to cool them quickly. Shell them carefully (they will be fragile), pat dry, cut in half and arrange on a plate.

Sprinkle the eggs with a little salt, the parsley and garlic. Grind on some black pepper then sieve over a little paprika and garnish with the olives, if you are using them. Drizzle with a little oil and serve immediately with good crusty bread.

Fried asparagus

Asparagi fritti

You've probably had asparagus every which way except coated in parmesan cheese and fried! These are so deliciously scrumptious that you'd better make plenty. If you like, serve them with a light salad – interesting leaves garnished with extra virgin olive oil, lemon juice, salt and pepper.

2 small eggs
salt
freshly ground black pepper to
  taste
freshly grated nutmeg
500g (1lb 2oz) stubby
  asparagus spears, trimmed
  and washed
50g (2oz) Dried white
  breadcrumbs, preferably
  homemade (see page 114)
3 tbsp freshly grated parmesan
  cheese, plus extra for serving
olive oil for frying

SERVES 4

Break the eggs into a shallow dish. Whisk in ¼ teaspoon of salt, plenty of black pepper and some nutmeg. Let the egg mixture settle for 10 minutes, then beat it together again (the salt thins the eggs, making it easier to coat the asparagus). Add the asparagus and shake the dish to coat the spears with the beaten egg.

Spread the breadcrumbs on a large plate and mix the parmesan cheese and ½ teaspoon of salt through them. Have ready a large heavy-based frying pan with olive oil to a depth of 5mm (⅕ in) set over a medium-high heat. When the oil is hot, drain the asparagus of excess egg and transfer to the breadcrumbs. Coat each spear evenly with the crumbs and lower them carefully into the hot oil (cook about eight at a time). Fry the spears until they are golden, then carefully turn and cook the second side.

Transfer the fried spears to a plate lined with absorbent kitchen paper to drain. Place onto a clean plate, sprinkle with a little extra parmesan cheese and serve immediately.

Steamed mussels with basil dressing
Muscoli al vapore con basilico

Garlic, parsley and basil add a level of complexity to the fresh sea tang in this dish of steamed mussels. In Italy you would use the small, black Mediterranean mussels but you might like to try it with the green shell variety.

1 clove garlic, crushed
2 tbsp chopped parsley
2 tbsp chopped basil
3 tbsp olive oil
2 tbsp white wine
3 tbsp white wine vinegar
few pinches of salt
freshly ground black pepper
24 small mussels, cleaned (see
  page 13)

SERVES 2–4

Put the garlic, parsley and basil in a large, shallow saucepan with the olive oil. Sauté for 2–3 minutes over a medium heat, then increase the heat to high and add the white wine, white wine vinegar, salt and black pepper. Tip in the mussels and cover the pan with a lid. Cook for 3–5 minutes, stirring occasionally, until the mussels open. Reject any that do not open.

Transfer the mussels to a warm dish as soon as they are done, then pour over the juices (if the juices are gritty, strain them first). Serve hot or at room temperature.

Bruschetta with chickpea pâté and barbecued tomatoes

Bruschetta con pâté di ceci e pomodori grigliati

This is a modern adaptation of a rustic treatment for bread. The sweet tomatoes set against the mealy taste of chickpeas, biting zing of garlic and fresh flavours of mint, make this a delectable nibble.

300g (10oz) can chickpeas, drained and rinsed
salt
2 tbsp lemon juice, strained
2 cloves garlic, (crush one, leave one whole)
freshly ground black pepper to taste
extra virgin olive oil
1 tbsp finely chopped parsley
1 tbsp finely chopped mint, plus sprigs for garnishing
6 firm vine-ripened or outdoor tomatoes, halved
caster sugar
ciabatta loaf, sliced (or use French bread)

SERVES 6–8

Put the chickpeas in a food processor with ¼ teaspoon salt, the lemon juice, crushed garlic, black pepper and 1 tablespoon of extra virgin olive oil. Add 1 tablespoon of water and process until smooth, adding a little extra water if the mixture is too thick. Transfer to a bowl and blend in the parsley and mint. Cover and chill until required (this can be made up to a day in advance); bring to room temperature before serving.

When ready to prepare the bruschetta, cook the tomatoes first, then the bread. Brush the skin side of the tomatoes with oil, put them on a plate, sprinkle the cut side with salt then dust with caster sugar. Cook on a heated barbecue grill, cut side down, until lightly browned. Turn and quickly cook the second side then transfer to a plate.

Toast the slices of bread over a heated barbecue grill or in the oven. Transfer to a board, rub each slice with the cut clove of garlic, drizzle on a little extra virgin olive oil and sprinkle with salt. Spread the chickpea pâté on the bruschetta and top each slice with a roasted tomato and a mint leaf. Serve immediately.

Mozzarella and roasted red pepper salad Insalata di mozzarella e peperoni

Bocconcini means "little mouthful" and it is used to describe small balls of fresh mozzarella sold in whey. The bland, milky taste of fresh mozzarella cheese is a perfect foil for the sweetness of roasted red peppers. Serve this with olives and bread as an antipasto dish.

3 large red peppers, roasted
  (see page 10)
150g (5oz) mozzarella
  bocconcini in whey, drained
few fresh basil leaves, torn into
  small pieces
1 tbsp balsamic vinegar
¼ teaspoon salt
freshly ground black pepper
  to taste
1 clove garlic, crushed
2 tbsp capers, drained
4 tbsp extra virgin olive oil

SERVES 4–6

Thinly slice the red peppers and set aside with the juices. Pat the mozzarella balls dry with absorbent kitchen paper, then slice them thinly with a sharp knife and arrange on a serving platter with the prepared peppers. Scatter the torn basil leaves over the top.

In a bowl, blend the balsamic vinegar, salt, black pepper, crushed garlic, capers and extra virgin olive oil. Mix in any reserved pepper juices. Pour over the mozzarella balls and peppers, toss gently and serve immediately.

Bruschetta with tomato and orange

Bruschetta con arance e pomodoro

Tomatoes are at their peak when they have had plenty of summer sun on them to sweeten their juices. Try them sliced on bruschetta, topped with juicy chunks of orange.

ciabatta loaf
2 fresh cloves garlic, peeled
12 ripe outdoor tomatoes, sliced
6 juicy oranges, sliced
extra virgin olive oil (choose an estate-bottled oil with a fruity taste)
salt and freshly ground black pepper to taste

SERVES 6

To make bruschetta, slice the ciabatta and toast the slices on a barbecue or under the grill. Rub the bruschetta with a cut clove of garlic and arrange sliced tomatoes and oranges on top. Drizzle with oil, grind on some pepper and sprinkle with salt. Serve immediately.

Parmesan with rocket leaves

Parmigiano e rucola

A few snippets of peppery rocket leaves strewn on a plate, topped with curls of piquant parmesan cheese and drizzled with extra virgin olive oil (mortgage your house to buy the best available) – what a clever dish!

2–3 good handfuls of rocket leaves, washed, dried and torn into bite-sized pieces
slab of parmesan cheese
extra virgin olive oil

SERVES 4

Put the rocket leaves on a serving platter. Shave the parmesan cheese into curls with a potato peeler and arrange on top of the rocket leaves. Drizzle with extra virgin olive oil and serve immediately.

Minestrone soup
Minestrone

Every region in Italy has a version of minestrone, made with a selection of the locally available vegetables and herbs, thickened and enriched with rice, beans or pasta. Try to make the soup the day before you intend serving it, as the flavours will fuse together making for a tastier dish. It will keep for three days in the refrigerator or it can be frozen.

3 tbsp olive oil
2 medium onions, finely chopped
2 large cloves garlic, crushed
150g (5oz) bacon, rind removed, finely chopped (optional)
1 tbsp finely chopped fresh marjoram (or 1 tsp dried)
1 tsp finely chopped fresh thyme (or ½ tsp dried)
400g (14oz) can Italian tomatoes, mashed
150g (5oz) small, dried white beans, soaked overnight in
  cold water, drained and rinsed
3L (5pt) stock (use light stock, or vegetable water, or 1 stock
  cube dissolved in water)
2 carrots, peeled and finely sliced
2 sticks celery, finely sliced
2 medium potatoes, peeled and diced
400g (14oz) pumpkin, peeled, chopped and seeds removed
250g (9oz) cauliflower florets, chopped
2 green or yellow courgettes, cut into thick rounds
salt
150g (5oz) spinach, chopped
100g (4oz) freshly grated parmesan cheese
2 tbsp pesto (or 2 tbsp finely chopped basil)

SERVES 10

Heat the olive oil in a large saucepan and add the onions, garlic and bacon, if using. Cook gently for 10 minutes or until the bacon fat starts to run. Add the marjoram and thyme, cook for 1 minute more, then add the tomatoes, beans and stock. Bring to the boil, partially cover with a lid, and simmer gently for 1–2 hours or until the beans are tender.

Add the carrots and celery, bring back to a gentle boil and cook gently for 20 minutes. Add the potatoes, pumpkin, cauliflower, courgettes and 1 teaspoon of salt. Bring back to the boil and cook gently for about 30 minutes or until the vegetables are very tender. Lastly, add the spinach and simmer for 15 minutes. Check the seasoning, adding more salt if necessary.

If not for immediate consumption, cool the pot of soup quickly in a sink filled with cold water, then refrigerate. Reheat gently. When hot, swirl in 3 table-spoons of the parmesan cheese. Spoon the pesto on top of the soup, then ladle it into bowls and serve with the remaining cheese. (If using chopped basil leaves, swirl through the soup with the parmesan cheese.)

Fish soup
Brodetto

This recipe is based on a substantial fish soup, which is more of a main course fish stew. Use white fish fillets for a delicate flavour and meatier fish fillets for a more robust dish. Do go to the effort of making your own fish stock for the soup – it adds a layer of flavour.

4 tbsp extra virgin olive oil
3 large cloves garlic, crushed
6 heaped tbsp chopped parsley
400g (14oz) can Italian tomatoes,
  well mashed
½ large green pepper, finely
  chopped
freshly ground black pepper to taste
1 tsp salt
250ml (8fl oz) Fish stock
  (see page 115)
1kg (2¼lb) assorted fish fillets, rinsed
  (include a few steamed mussels, see
  page 13, and small green prawns
  if you like)

Croûtes
French bread or focaccia,
  thinly sliced
extra virgin olive oil
1 clove garlic, peeled and halved

SERVES 4

Put the extra virgin olive oil in a wide saucepan with the garlic and parsley. Cook over a gentle heat, stirring, until the garlic just starts to change colour. Add the tomatoes and the green pepper. Cook gently for 10 minutes, then grind on some black pepper and add the salt.

Pour in the stock and bring to the boil. Cook gently for 10 minutes, then add the fish fillets. Partially cover with a lid and cook very gently for about 7 minutes or until the fish is just cooked through. If you are using mussels and prawns, add them during the last few minutes and cook until the prawns turn pink throughout (about 2 minutes).

Meanwhile, make the garlic croûtes. Brush the bread with olive oil and place on a baking tray. Toast in an oven preheated to 180°C/350°F/gas 4 for 7–10 minutes or until they are golden. Remove the croûtes from the oven and immediately rub each slice generously with the cut clove of garlic.

Ladle the soup into hot bowls and serve with the warm garlic croûtes.

Pasta

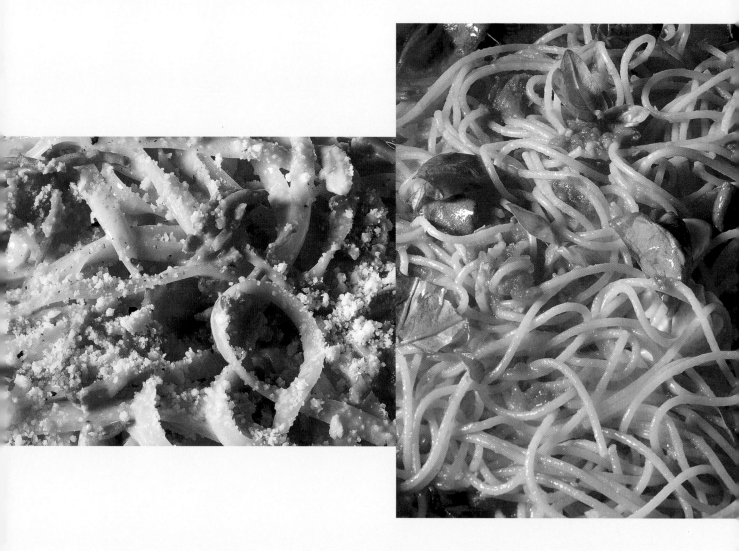

Crab and lemon pasta
Pasta con granchi e limone

This sauce is light and lemony, despite it being made with cream, and it belongs on delicate pasta. The green peppercorns burst on the palate and lift the flavour.

250g (9oz) pasta (such as fettuccine
  or linguine)
salt
300ml (½pt) single cream
zest of 2 lemons
freshly ground black pepper to taste
1 tbsp green peppercorns, drained
sea salt
250g (9oz) fresh crabmeat (if
  frozen, thaw, then squeeze out
  excess moisture by hand)
2 tbsp chopped flat leaf parsley
sautéed crab claws, to garnish
  (optional)

SERVES 4 AS A STARTER,
2 AS A MAIN COURSE

Cook the pasta in plenty of gently boiling, well-salted water until al dente; this will only take a few minutes, so you should have everything co-ordinated before putting the pasta on to cook.

Meanwhile, put the cream, lemon zest, black pepper, green peppercorns and a good pinch of sea salt in a small pan and heat gently. Reduce by a quarter.

When the pasta is nearly ready, add the crabmeat to the cream sauce. Cook for a few minutes more, add the parsley and check the seasoning.

Drain the pasta, turn it into a heated serving bowl and pour the crab sauce over. Toss well and serve immediately in hot pasta bowls. Garnish with crab claws if you like.

Jumping spaghetti

Spaghetti saltati

That's what the spaghetti does – it jumps in the pan when it is tossed with the delicious fresh tomato sauce.

4 large outdoor or vine-
   ripened tomatoes, skinned
3 tbsp extra virgin olive oil
4 cloves garlic, halved
salt
3 tbsp chopped basil
350g (12oz) spaghetti
knob of butter
2–3 small dried "bird's eye"
   chillies, crushed (optional)
freshly grated parmesan
   cheese to serve

SERVES 4 AS A STARTER

Halve the tomatoes, remove the cores and flick out the seeds. Chop the flesh very finely until pulpy.

Put the extra virgin olive oil in a large heavy-based frying pan and add the garlic. Cook gently until golden, then remove with a slotted spoon and discard. Take the pan off the heat, carefully tip in the tomatoes and stir well. Return the pan to the heat and cook the tomatoes gently, uncovered, for 20 minutes, or until sauce-like. Add ¼ teaspoon of salt and the basil and turn off the heat.

Cook the pasta in plenty of gently boiling, well-salted water until nearly al dente. Drain.

Set the frying pan back over a medium-high heat and add the butter and the chillies, if using. Mix well, then tip the spaghetti into the pan. Heat through for 1 minute, tossing, then transfer to hot pasta bowls. Serve immediately with plenty of parmesan cheese.

Lasagnette with Italian sausage and mushroom ragù
Lasagnette con ragù di salsiccia e funghi

There's nothing subtle about this sauce with its chunky texture and robust flavour, which is dependent on well-made sausages.

3 tbsp extra virgin olive oil
1 onion, very finely chopped
250g (9oz) button
  mushrooms, sliced
freshly ground black pepper
  to taste
250g (9oz) Italian-style
  sausages (use meaty,
  well-seasoned sausages)
2 bay leaves
600g (1¼lb) canned Italian
  tomatoes, mashed
salt
500g (1lb 2oz) lasagnette
  (small curly-edged pieces of
  lasagne, or use fusilli
  or cavatappi)
freshly grated parmesan
  cheese for serving

SERVES 6 AS A STARTER,
4 AS A MAIN COURSE

Heat the extra virgin olive oil in a heavy-based saucepan over a low-to-medium heat and add the onion. Cook until it is a light golden colour, then increase the heat to medium-high and add the mushrooms. Stir to coat them in the onion-flavoured oil, then grind on some black pepper.

Meanwhile, prepare the sausages. Split the skin and discard it, then chop the sausage meat (a bit messy, but necessary).

Add the sausage meat to the pan, increase the heat to high and cook for 2–3 minutes, stirring, and breaking up the meat with a large fork. Add the bay leaves and tomatoes. Bring to the boil and add a few pinches of salt. Turn the heat to low, partially cover with a lid and simmer gently for about 30 minutes (break up the sausage meat with a fork as it cooks). The sauce should end up looking like a ragù (meat sauce), moist but not dry.

Meanwhile, cook the pasta in plenty of gently boiling, well-salted water until al dente. Drain briefly and turn into a heated serving dish. Pour the sauce over, toss well and serve immediately with parmesan cheese.

Tart's spaghetti
Spaghetti alla puttanesca

This dish may have a shady origin, but without a doubt, it's the most loved pasta dish I've ever put in print. People rave about it and I often return to it myself, because it's got everything a good pasta dish should have: the ingredients are usually close at hand, it's quick to cook, it fills the kitchen with hunger-inducing aromas and it tastes so good, I can't live without it!

75ml (2½ fl oz) extra virgin olive oil
2 cloves garlic, crushed
75g (3oz) can anchovies, drained
　　and mashed (optional)
2 small dried "bird's eye"
　　chillies, crushed (optional)
600g (1¼lb) canned Italian
　　tomatoes, mashed
2 tbsp Italian tomato purée
1 tbsp capers, drained (if large, chop them)
1 tbsp finely chopped fresh oregano
　　(or 1 tsp dried)
salt
freshly ground black pepper to taste
50g (2oz) black olives (approximately 10),
　　pitted and chopped
500g (1lb 2oz) spaghetti
　　(or use spaghettini, penne, or rigatoni)
freshly grated parmesan cheese for serving

SERVES 6 AS A STARTER, 4 AS A MAIN COURSE

Put the oil in a heavy-based pan, set over a medium heat. Add the garlic. Sauté until it turns a pale biscuit colour, then stir in the anchovies and chillies, if using.

Carefully tip in the tomatoes, the tomato purée, capers, oregano, a few large pinches of salt and some black pepper (omit the salt if you are adding the anchovies; check the seasoning once the sauce is cooked). Bring the sauce to the boil, lower the heat and cook gently, stirring occasionally, for 25–30 minutes or until the tomatoes are pulpy. Add the olives.

Meanwhile, cook the pasta in gently boiling, well-salted water until al dente. Drain briefly and turn it into a heated serving dish. Pour three-quarters of the sauce over the pasta, toss together, then top with the rest of the sauce. Serve immediately with parmesan cheese.

Fettuccine with Roman style meat sauce

Fettuccine alla romana

This rich meaty sauce works with fettuccine and chunky types of pasta such as rigatoni.

1 small onion, very finely chopped
1 small carrot, very finely chopped
1 stick celery, very finely chopped
75g (3oz) bacon, rind removed,
   finely chopped
50g (2oz) butter, plus extra for
   tossing through pasta
300g (10oz) prime minced beef
salt
freshly ground black pepper to taste
freshly grated nutmeg
100g (4oz) chicken livers, rinsed,
   trimmed and finely chopped
75ml (2½ fl oz) dry red wine
600g (1¼ lb) canned Italian
   tomatoes, mashed
1½ tbsp Italian tomato purée
½ tsp sugar
¼ tsp dried oregano
500g (1lb 2oz) fettuccine
knob of butter
freshly grated parmesan cheese
   for serving

SERVES 6 AS A STARTER,
4 AS A MAIN COURSE

Put the onion, carrot, celery and bacon in a saucepan with the butter. Fry gently until the onion is a pale golden colour. Increase the heat to high and add the minced beef. Break the beef up with a fork and cook until it loses its pinkness. Season with ¼ teaspoon of salt, some black pepper and some nutmeg. Add the chicken livers and cook for a further 2 minutes.

Turn the heat down to medium, stir in the wine and cook until it has evaporated. Add the tomatoes, tomato purée, sugar and oregano. Bring to the boil, then lower the heat and cook gently, uncovered, for 30 minutes. Partially cover with a lid and cook for 15–30 minutes more, stirring occasionally, until rich and thick.

Cook the pasta in plenty of gently boiling, well-salted water until al dente. Drain briefly and turn into a heated serving dish. Quickly toss a large knob of butter through, then pour the sauce over (don't toss). Serve immediately with parmesan cheese.

Rigatoni with tomato sauce
Rigatoni con sugo di pomodoro

Tomato sauce is the quintessential pasta sauce served throughout Italy. Other ingredients can be added for variation, but this idea – culled from my Italian family – is one of my favourites.

75ml (2½ fl oz) extra virgin olive oil
3 large cloves garlic, crushed
2 x 400g (14oz) cans Italian
  tomatoes, mashed
2 tbsp Italian tomato purée
freshly ground black pepper to taste
salt
2 large aubergines
olive oil
500g (1lb 2oz) rigatoni
  (or elicoidali, penne or penne ziti)
freshly grated parmesan cheese
  for serving

SERVES 6 AS A STARTER,
4 AS A MAIN COURSE

Put the extra virgin olive oil and garlic in a heavy-based saucepan and cook gently until it turns a pale biscuit colour. Carefully pour in the tomatoes. Add the tomato purée, some black pepper and ½ teaspoon of salt. Rinse the tomato cans with a little water (a frugal Italian trick, making sure nothing is wasted!), using about 175ml (6fl oz) of water in total, and add the water to the pan of sauce.

Bring the sauce to the boil, then cook, uncovered, for 30–35 minutes or until reduced and pulpy.

Meanwhile, slice the aubergines into rounds about 5mm (⅕in) thick. Pat dry with absorbent kitchen paper. Heat a good depth of oil (about 2.5cm/1in deep) in a large heavy-based frying pan over a high heat until it gives off a haze.

Carefully slide in as many slices of aubergine as will fit in one layer and cook until they are a rich golden brown on both sides. Transfer to a plate lined with absorbent kitchen paper and sprinkle lightly with salt. Repeat the process with the rest of the aubergine slices.

When the sauce and aubergine are ready (both can be prepared in advance), cook the pasta in plenty of gently boiling, well-salted water until al dente. Drain briefly then turn the pasta into a heated serving dish. Toss three-quarters of the sauce through the pasta. Spoon the rest of the sauce on top and serve immediately with the aubergine slices (which are best served hottish) and plenty of grated parmesan cheese.

Spaghettini with tomato sauce, chilli and saffron prawns

Spaghettini con pomodoro, peperoncino e gamberi allo zafferano

My brother-in-law Ferruccio introduced me to chilled pasta dishes. The thing about this dish is that it doesn't seem to matter whether it is served hot, hottish, at room temperature or even chilled; it's always fantastic.

500g (1lb 2oz) vine-ripened
   tomatoes
1 large clove garlic, crushed
2 tbsp coarsely chopped flat leaf
   parsley
2 tbsp small basil leaves
salt
4 small dried "bird's eye"
   chillies, crushed
12 black olives, pitted
   and chopped
3 tbsp estate-bottled extra virgin
   olive oil plus a little regular extra
   virgin olive oil for frying
   the prawns
24 raw prawns
pinch saffron strands
400g (14oz) spaghettini
   (or spaghetti)

SERVES 4

Skin the tomatoes and cut them in half. Remove the cores and flick out the seeds. Chop the flesh into tiny dice, then put the tomatoes in a sieve set over a bowl. Leave to drain for 1 hour. Transfer the tomatoes to a bowl and mix in the garlic, parsley, basil leaves, 1/2 teaspoon of salt, two of the crushed chillies, the olives and estate-bottled extra virgin olive oil. Set aside while preparing the prawns and pasta.

Twist the heads off the prawns and peel away the shells, leaving the small piece of shell on the tail intact. Slit down the back of each prawn with a sharp knife and gently extract the black or orangey-red vein running right down the length. Rinse the prawns and pat dry with kitchen paper.

Heat a drizzle of extra virgin oil in a small frying pan over a medium heat. Add the prawns and cook until pink. Turn them, crumble the saffron and the last two chillies on top and cook until pink on the other side. Transfer to a small bowl with any scrapings from the pan.

Meanwhile, cook the pasta in plenty of gently boiling, well-salted water until al dente. Drain and tip into a heated serving dish. Pour the sauce over and quickly toss together. Tip the prawns on top and serve hottish or at room temperature.

Fettuccine with courgettes

Fettuccine con zucchine

The contrast of delicate pasta with crispy batons of fried courgettes is sensational. This is not a difficult dish to make, just ensure you start with small courgettes, not big watery ones full of seeds.

750g (1lb 10oz) small, firm
  courgettes
salt
75g (3oz) plain flour
olive oil
freshly ground black pepper
  to taste
2 large cloves garlic, chopped
  (use mild, new season garlic)
1 tbsp chopped fresh
  marjoram
500g (1lb 2oz) pasta such as
  fettuccine
50g (2oz) butter
handful of basil leaves, torn
  into small pieces
50g (2oz) freshly grated
  parmesan cheese, plus extra
  for serving

SERVES 4

Cut the courgettes into fat matchsticks. Put in a colander and toss with a teaspoon of salt. Leave to drain for 1 hour, then gently squeeze to push out as much water as possible. Wrap the courgette sticks in absorbent kitchen paper and get them as dry as possible.

Put half the flour on a double thickness of kitchen paper and add half the courgette sticks. Toss them in the flour until they are coated.

Have ready a pan with hot olive oil to a depth of 5mm (⅕in) set over a medium-high heat. When the oil is nice and hot, drop in the courgettes. Cook quickly until golden brown on both sides, then transfer them to a colander to drain. Sprinkle with a little salt and grind on some black pepper. Repeat the process with the rest of the courgettes. Add the garlic to the pan for the last 2–3 minutes of cooking, until it is a pale golden colour, then scatter the marjoram over. Transfer the contents of the pan to the colander with the first batch of courgettes.

Meanwhile, cook the pasta until al dente; if using dried pasta, put it into the water once you've cooked the first batch of courgettes but, if using fresh pasta, which cooks more quickly, put it in the water when the second half of the courgettes is nearly cooked. Drain the pasta, then turn it into a very hot bowl. Mix the butter, basil, some black pepper and the parmesan cheese through the pasta. Toss quickly, then top with the courgettes. Toss briefly and serve immediately in hot bowls.

Summer pasta salad

Insalata di pasta estiva

Pasta salads – when well made – are light and delicious. This one is particularly good, capturing the essence of vine-ripened tomatoes, enhanced by garlic and lemon zest. For a change, top the salad with flakes of hot smoked salmon, a handful of baby basil, rocket leaves or all three!

300g (10oz) maltagliati Emilian
  egg pasta
salt
4 tbsp extra virgin olive oil
12 small vine-ripened
  tomatoes, halved
1 large clove garlic, crushed
2 tbsp salted capers, rinsed,
  soaked for 15 minutes, rinsed
  again and drained
zest of ½ a lemon
freshly ground black pepper
  to taste

SERVES 6

Cook the pasta in plenty of gently boiling, well-salted water until al dente.

While the pasta is cooking, put 1 tablespoon of the extra virgin olive oil in a frying pan and add the tomatoes. Cook very gently for about 10 minutes, to encourage the juices to run; don't let them fry. This can be done ahead.

Mix the remaining extra virgin olive oil, garlic, capers, lemon zest, black pepper and a few pinches of salt in a small bowl.

When the pasta is ready, drain it and tip into a large bowl. Pour the dressing over and toss well, then tip the tomatoes on, with all their juices. Toss carefully. The pasta can be served hottish or at room temperature.

Baked rigatoni with ricotta

Rigatoni con ricotta al forno

This is an excellent dish to have in your repertoire because everyone loves it, including me. It's filling but not rich, is well-flavoured and can be assembled ahead of time then cooked in the oven when required.

1 large onion, finely chopped
2 cloves garlic, crushed
75ml (2½fl oz) olive oil
1 tsp dried marjoram
freshly ground black pepper to taste
2 x 400g (14oz) cans Italian
 tomatoes, mashed
salt
500g (1lb 2oz) rigatoni (or use large pasta
 shells or other tubular pasta)
50g (2oz) butter
200g (7oz) ricotta cheese
50g (2oz) freshly grated parmesan cheese,
 plus extra for serving

SERVES 6

Put the onion and garlic in a heavy-based saucepan with the olive oil and cook gently until lightly golden. Add the marjoram and black pepper, then tip the tomatoes in and add ½ teaspoon of salt. Bring to the boil, then turn the heat to very low. Cook, uncovered, stirring occasionally, for about 25 minutes or until the sauce is pulpy.

Cook the pasta in plenty of gently boiling, well-salted water until nearly al dente (don't overcook the pasta because it continues to cook in the oven).

Preheat the oven to 180°C/350°F/gas 4. Drain the pasta well and turn it into a large bowl. Toss half of the butter and 3 tablespoons of the sauce through. Tip half the pasta into a well-buttered ovenproof dish (33 x 21 x 5cm/13 x 8¼ x 2in deep). Spoon a little sauce over it, then spoon the ricotta cheese on, then coat with a little more sauce. Sprinkle half the parmesan cheese over, then put the rest of the pasta in the dish. Spoon the remaining sauce over the top, sprinkle with the rest of the parmesan cheese and dot with butter. (The pasta can be prepared an hour or two in advance to this point; cover loosely with waxed paper and keep at room temperature.)

Bake in the oven for 15–20 minutes, or until piping hot and a little crusty on top. Serve immediately with extra parmesan cheese.

Fettuccine with creamy bacon sauce Fettuccine alla carbonara

This Roman dish of pasta with bacon, eggs and cream makes a substantial main course dish. It's easy enough to make, but ensure you get everything ready before you start to cook the sauce. It is traditionally made with spaghetti, but in our household we enjoy it made with fettuccine. We also like it with extra cheese.

300g (10oz) (approximately 8 rashers) smoked bacon, rind removed, cut into small strips
50g (2oz) soft butter
2 eggs
2 egg yolks
120g (4½ oz) freshly grated parmesan cheese
freshly ground black pepper to taste
500g (1lb 2oz) fettuccine
salt
150ml (¼ pt) single cream

SERVES 4

Heat a large frying pan over a medium heat. When hot, add the bacon. Cook, stirring occasionally, until very crisp. Drain off most of the visible fat and turn off the heat.

Bring a large saucepan of water to the boil. Place an ovenproof serving dish in a warm oven and allow it to get very hot (choose a dish that will hold the heat well, such as thick pottery, chunky china or cast iron).

Cream the butter in a small bowl with a spatula until it is very soft. Put the eggs, egg yolks and half the parmesan cheese into another small bowl. Beat well with a fork, adding black pepper to taste.

Cook the pasta in plenty of gently boiling, well-salted water until al dente.

Meanwhile, reheat the bacon in the pan, add the cream and bubble it up. Drain the pasta and transfer it to the very hot dish. Immediately work the butter through with two large spoons. Add the hot bacon mixture, then the eggs and cheese. Toss vigorously and serve immediately with the remaining cheese. (The heat of the ingredients and the dish will be sufficient to cook the eggs, but the mixture should remain light, not tacky or scrambled.)

Risotto, Polenta and Pies

Easter pie Torta Pasqualina

This pie, an Easter speciality, was originally made with 33 layers of pastry, representing Christ's age at the time of his crucifixion. I use filo pastry in place of olive oil dough, as it not only saves time but also produces an appetizingly crisp result.

2 tbsp olive oil
1 large onion, finely chopped
2 x 400g (14oz) cans
   artichoke hearts, drained
freshly ground black pepper
   to taste
350g (12oz) ricotta cheese
175ml (6fl oz) milk
pinch of salt
about 100g (4oz) butter
350g (12oz) packet
   filo pastry
8 eggs
freshly ground black pepper
   to taste
1 tbsp finely chopped
   fresh marjoram
   (or ½ tbsp dried)
75g (3oz) freshly grated
   parmesan cheese

SERVES 8

Heat the olive oil in a frying pan over a medium heat and add the onion. Cook until lightly golden, stirring occasionally.

Squeeze all the brine from the artichokes, chop them roughly and add to the onion. Cook for 3–4 minutes, stirring, until any moisture is driven off. Grind over plenty of black pepper, then cool.

Put the ricotta cheese in a bowl and beat until smooth, then blend in the milk by degrees. Add a pinch of salt and the artichoke mixture. Mix well.

Melt most of the butter. Lay the first sheet of filo pastry on a clean, dry surface and brush lightly with the butter, then lay a second sheet on top and brush it with butter, too. Continue layering buttered sheets of filo in this way until 11 sheets of pastry are stacked up. Mould the buttered sheets into a buttered rectangular dish, about 32 x 21 x 5cm (12½ x 8¼ x 2in), and carefully trim off any over-hanging pastry.

Spoon in the ricotta mixture and use a large metal spoon to make eight hollows in it. Crack the eggs, one by one, into a small dish and then drop them into the hollows. Put 2–3 small dots of butter on each egg, grind some black pepper over and sprinkle with the marjoram and parmesan cheese.

Prepare another 11 sheets of filo in the way described and place these on top of the pie. Gently press in place, then trim off any overhanging pastry.

Brush the top lightly with butter and bake in an oven preheated to 200°C/400°F/gas 6 for about 40 minutes or until the filo is a rich golden colour on top (lower the heat if necessary to prevent over-browning or place a piece of aluminium foil over the top of the pie). Allow it to cool slightly before cutting into wedges.

Aubergine pie

Torta di melanzane

Serve this rich and filling classic Neapolitan dish with a salad of mixed leaves and fresh, crusty bread. You will have tomato sauce left over. Refrigerate and use within 3 days or freeze it for later use.

2–3 medium aubergines
(about 600g/1¼ lb total)
plain flour
olive oil for frying
250ml (8fl oz) Chunky tomato
sauce (see page 116)
small handful of basil leaves
salt
150g (5oz) mozzarella
bocconcini in whey,
drained and sliced
50g (2oz) freshly grated
parmesan cheese

SERVES 6–8

Cut the aubergines into thin slices and dust about a third of them with flour. Heat 120ml (4fl oz) of olive oil in a frying pan over a medium-high heat. When the oil is very hot, put in a single layer of aubergine slices. Fry on both sides to a rich golden brown, lift out and drain on a plate lined with crumpled absorbent kitchen paper. Continue cooking the rest of the aubergine slices, dusting them with flour first and adding more oil when necessary. Alternatively, oven-bake the aubergine slices, according to the instructions on page 115.

Lightly grease a medium-sized ovenproof dish and put in a layer of aubergine slices. Top each aubergine slice with a teaspoonful of tomato sauce, half a basil leaf, a light sprinkling of salt and a slice of mozzarella. Sprinkle some parmesan cheese over. Continue layering the pie in this way, ending with a layer of aubergine slices and a generous sprinkling of parmesan cheese.

Bake the pie in an oven preheated to 180°C/350°F/gas 4 for 30–40 minutes, or until it is a rich golden colour on top. Cool for 10 minutes in the dish before serving. (If the juices appear watery, pour them off; they should be dark and richly flavoured.)

Spinach torte   Torta di spinaci

This is another beauty from my Emilian sister-in-law, Isanna. It can be prepared several hours ahead but it is best served hottish or at room temperature. If you have any leftovers, keep them refrigerated, but bring to room temperature before serving.

500g (1lb 2oz) spinach, trimmed and washed well
250g (9oz) Italian rice – arborio, vialone nano, carnaroli
salt
butter
3 tbsp olive oil
1 large onion, finely chopped
1 large clove garlic, crushed
freshly ground black pepper to taste
freshly grated nutmeg
4 eggs, lightly beaten
1 tsp finely chopped sage (or a few pinches of dried)
75g (3oz) freshly grated parmesan cheese
extra butter, melted

SERVES 6–8

Bring 750ml (1¼pt) of water to the boil in a large saucepan. Plunge in the spinach, pushing it under the water with a wooden spoon, and cook until wilted. Drain and refresh with cold water, then drain again. Press out as much moisture as possible, then chop with a knife.

Tip the rice into a saucepan of salted water. Bring to the boil, then cook gently, uncovered, for 10 minutes. Drain, then return to the rinsed and dried saucepan. Stir in a large knob of butter.

Meanwhile, put the olive oil in a frying pan with the onion. Cook over a gentle heat until lightly golden. Add the garlic and cook for another minute, then tip the mixture into the rice. Grind over plenty of black pepper and nutmeg and add ½ teaspoon of salt. Pour in the eggs and add the spinach, sage and most of the parmesan cheese.

With a large fork blend the mixture together, then turn it into a buttered, loose-bottomed 20cm (7¾in) diameter cake tin (line the base with buttered baking parchment or blanched spinach leaves). Drizzle the surface with a little melted butter. Sprinkle the rest of the cheese over the top. The torte can be prepared a few hours in advance to this point; cover and keep at room temperature for up to 1 hour, otherwise refrigerate it (bring to room temperature before cooking).

Bake in an oven preheated to 200°C/400°F/gas 6 for about 25 minutes or until the top is crisp. Rest for 5 minutes, then loosen from the sides of the tin, invert and lift off the base of the tin (peel off the parchment, if using). Serve hot or warm.

Oven-baked aubergine risotto

Risotto con melanzane al forno

Try the next two oven-baked layered risotto dishes; they're quicker and can be prepared in advance.

2 medium-large aubergines
  (about 250g/9oz each)
250ml (8fl oz) olive oil
  for frying
750ml (1¼pt) light stock
2 tbsp olive oil
25g (1oz) butter, plus
  a little extra
1 small onion, finely chopped
2 cloves garlic, crushed
400g (14oz) can Italian
  tomatoes, mashed
2 tbsp finely chopped basil
salt
freshly ground black pepper
  to taste
250g (9oz) Italian rice –
  arborio, vialone nano,
  carnaroli
120ml (4fl oz) dry white wine
50g (2oz) freshly grated
  parmesan cheese
150g (5oz) mozzarella
  bocconcini in whey, drained
  and cubed

SERVES 4

Slice the aubergines into large rounds about 5mm (⅕ in) thick. Heat the frying oil in a large frying pan until it is hot and lightly smoking. Put in several slices of aubergine and cook until they are golden brown. Turn with tongs and cook the other side. Drain on absorbent kitchen paper. Repeat with the remaining aubergine slices. Alternatively, bake the aubergine slices as instructed on page 115.

Make the risotto next. Bring the stock to a simmer, then set the heat so that it is kept very hot, but does not boil and evaporate. Put the olive oil and half the butter in a heavy-based saucepan over a medium heat, add the onion and garlic and sauté until a pale golden colour. Tip in the tomatoes and add the basil, ½ teaspoon of salt and some black pepper. Cook gently, uncovered, for 10 minutes, then pour all but 120ml (4fl oz) of the mixture into a bowl and set aside.

Add the rice to the tomato mixture in the pan. Increase the temperature to medium-high and stir for 2–3 minutes. Pour in the wine and cook, stirring, until it has nearly evaporated. Start adding the stock as described in the recipe for Basic risotto (see page 120) and cook until the rice is three-quarters cooked.

Layer the ingredients in a greased ovenproof dish (about 16–18cm/6¼–7in diameter and 8–9cm/3–3½in deep) in this order: rice, parmesan cheese, aubergine slices, tomato mixture and mozzarella. Finish with a top layer of rice, then parmesan cheese. (The dish can be prepared ahead to this point, refrigerated, then cooked when required, but it must be brought to room temperature before cooking.)

Dot the top with butter and bake in an oven preheated to 200°C/400°F/gas 6 for about 15 minutes until it is crisp on top and heated through. Allow to stand for 5 minutes before serving.

Oven-baked mushroom risotto
Risotto con funghi al forno

Which is my favourite? This baked risotto dish with the forest-floor scents of mushrooms or the previous one with the silky richness of aubergine? A hard choice – I love them both!

4 tbsp butter
500g (1lb 2oz) open-cup
   portabello mushrooms,
   wiped with a damp cloth
   and cut into thick slices
salt and freshly ground black
      pepper to taste
2 tbsp olive oil
1 small onion, finely chopped
2 cloves garlic, crushed
400g (14oz) can Italian
   tomatoes, mashed
2 tbsp finely chopped basil
1L (1³/₄ pt) vegetable stock
350g (12oz) Italian rice
100ml (3½ fl oz) dry
   white wine
50g (2oz) freshly grated
parmesan cheese
150g (5oz) mozzarella
   bocconcini in whey, drained
   and sliced

SERVES 4

Heat a large frying pan over a high heat. Add 2 tablespoons of butter and let it sizzle. Put in the mushrooms and cook, stirring, for 2–3 minutes; the butter will be absorbed and the pan will look dry. Season with salt and pepper, lower the heat and continue stirring until the juices start to run from the mushrooms. Increase the heat again and cook until most of the juice has evaporated.

Put the olive oil and 1 tablespoon of the butter in a heavy-based saucepan over a medium heat. Add the onion and garlic and sauté until a pale golden colour. Add the tomatoes, basil, ½ teaspoon of salt and some black pepper. Cook gently, uncovered, for 10 minutes, then pour all but 120ml (4fl oz) of the mixture into a bowl and set aside.

Meanwhile, bring the stock to a simmer, then set the heat so that it is kept very hot, but does not boil and evaporate.

Add rice to the tomato sauce in the pan. Increase the temperature to medium-high and stir for 2–3 minutes. Pour in the wine and cook, stirring, until it has nearly evaporated. Start adding stock a ladleful at a time. Continue cooking and adding stock as described in the recipe for Basic risotto (see page 120), until the rice is about three-quarters cooked. If you run out of stock, use hot water. Aim to finish with the rice sloppy but not soupy (it will take 15–18 minutes).

Layer the ingredients in a buttered ovenproof dish in this order: rice, parmesan cheese, mushrooms, tomato sauce and mozzarella. Finish with a top layer of rice and parmesan cheese. (The dish can be prepared ahead to this point, refrigerated, then cooked when required. It must be brought to room temperature before cooking.)

Dot the top with butter and bake in an oven preheated to 200°C/400°F/gas 6 for about 15 minutes, until it is crisp on top and heated through. Allow the risotto to stand for 5 minutes before serving. Accompany with a green salad.

Barbecued parmesan polenta with pine nuts and rosemary

Polenta alla griglia con pinoli e rosmarino

This is not what they do with polenta in Italy, but who cares! It's a fantastic recipe for a barbecue, it's got everything – you can prepare it ahead, it's got loads of flavour, it's filling and it's good for you. Omit the anchovies if you want to serve the dish to vegetarians.

1.2L (2pt) water
1 tsp salt
250g (9oz) polenta (use the instant variety, which cooks in 5 minutes)
25g (1oz) fresh butter
50g (2oz) freshly grated parmesan cheese
3 red peppers
1 yellow pepper
extra virgin olive oil
2 cloves garlic, chopped
1 tbsp chopped rosemary
100g (4oz) stoned and chopped black olives
3 anchovy fillets (buy anchovy fillets in oil), drained and squished (optional)
40g (1½oz) fresh pine nuts (old ones can be rancid)
olive oil
sea salt (optional)

SERVES 8 AS A STARTER,
6 AS A MAIN COURSE WITH SALAD

Bring the water to the boil in a large, wide (not tall and narrow) saucepan. Add the salt, then shake in the polenta from a height. Stir continuously, using a wooden spoon. When the polenta is cooked, (5 minutes for instant polenta or about 20 minutes if you use regular polenta), stir in the butter and parmesan cheese. Tip it onto a shallow tray and spread out to 1cm (⅓ in) thick. Smooth the surface and leave to cool. The cooked polenta can be stored for several hours at room temperature or it can be made a day in advance, but keep it covered and refrigerated until you are ready to use it.

Cook the peppers in hot coals or roast them in a very hot oven for about 20 minutes, until blackened and charred (see page 10). When cool, peel off the skins and slip out the cores and seeds, reserving any juices. Chop the peppers into fine strips. Heat 1 tablespoon of extra virgin olive oil over a low heat in a small pan and add the garlic and rosemary. Cook gently until aromatic, but don't let the garlic colour.

Add the black olives, take the pan off the heat then stir in the peppers and any juice. If using anchovies, blend them into the mixture. This can be prepared a few hours ahead; cover and keep it at room temperature.

Toast the pine nuts in a small dry pan or fry them in a little hot oil. (I prefer them fried in hot oil; move them around in the pan as they colour, turn them onto a plate lined with absorbent kitchen paper and sprinkle with sea salt.)

When ready to finish off the polenta, cut it into squares and brush it on both sides with olive oil.

Barbecue the pieces of polenta on a very hot barbecue grill, until lightly browned and crispy. Transfer to a serving platter. Spoon on the pepper topping and scatter pine nuts on top. Serve immediately with a good, interesting green salad.

Flaky ham and cheese pie
Scacciata

This pie, based on focaccia dough, has a soft, bready base, a thin crisp edge and a deliciously crunchy, flaky top.

1 batch Focaccia dough, made to end of Stage 2 (see page 118)
a little extra plain flour and olive oil

Filling
2 fleshy tomatoes, preferably plum tomatoes
1 medium onion, sliced into rings
150g (5oz) ham off the bone, cut into thin, short strips
100g (4oz) black olives, stoned and chopped
1 tsp dried oregano
freshly ground black pepper to taste
120g (4½ oz) emmenthal cheese, thinly sliced

SERVES 8

Cut the dough in half. Lightly flour one half and set it aside. Roll out the other half on a floured surface, dusting it with more flour to prevent sticking. If the dough is difficult to roll – if it keeps shrinking back after rolling – leave it to rest for 2–3 minutes. Roll out to about 32cm (12½ in) in diameter. Wrap the dough around a rolling pin and transfer it to a baking tray lined with a teflon baking sheet or baking parchment.

Next, make the filling. Cut a slice off the flower end of the tomatoes (the opposite end to the stalk or core end). Squeeze out most of the seeds and juice, then slice the tomatoes thinly. Scatter the onion rings over the dough, then add the tomatoes, ham and olives, keeping the mixture in slightly from the edges. Sprinkle the oregano over, grind on some black pepper and cover with emmenthal cheese.

Roll out the second half of the dough, wrap it around the rolling pin and unroll it gently on top of the pie. Press the edges of the dough together to seal, then crimp the edges with your fingers. Prick the surface all over with a fork, then brush with olive oil. Leave uncovered in a warm spot for 15 minutes.

Bake in an oven preheated to 200°C/400°F/gas 6 for 40–45 minutes or until it is golden brown on the top and bottom. Leave on the tray for 2–3 minutes, then carefully slide off onto a cooling rack. Cool for 5–10 minutes. Serve cut into large wedges.

Mediterranean pizza

Pizza Mediterranea

It's surprising how tasty a pizza can be with just a few well chosen ingredients. This pizza is a great way to use up leftover barbecued vegetables and fried artichokes.

1 large aubergine, sliced
olive oil
1 small yellow and red pepper, cored,
  seeded and cut into small chunks
120ml (4fl oz) passata or homemade or
  ready-prepared tomato sauce
1 Pizza dough base (see page 124)
20 fresh basil leaves
6 balls (150g/5oz) bocconcini
  mozzarella, drained and sliced
salt and freshly ground black pepper
  to taste
extra virgin olive oil

SERVES 2–4

Preheat the oven to 225°C/425°F/gas 7. Brush the aubergine slices with olive oil and bake them on an oiled baking sheet for about 20 minutes, or until a rich golden colour. The aubergine can be prepared ahead. Alternatively, cook the aubergine on the barbecue.

Put the chunks of pepper in a bowl and anoint with a little olive oil. Cook them on a hot barbecue plate or rack for about 10 minutes, or until lightly charred. Alternatively, fry them in hot oil until lightly browned and half-tender.

Smear dollops of passata or sauce on the pizza. Arrange the aubergine slices (halved if large), pepper and basil on top of the sauce, then the mozzarella. Sprinkle with salt, grind on some black pepper, drizzle with oil and bake as directed on page 124.

Flaky spinach pie   Erbazzone

I consider myself a bit of an erbazzone aficionado, having traipsed all over the streets of Reggio Emilia many a time with my sister-in-law Isanna, topping up our energy to keep shopping with slabs of this pie. I'm quite critical of the homemade version, but this one's a cracker – straight off Isanna's Emilian stove!

280g (9½oz) chopped, cooked, spinach (moisture squeezed out); (or use 500g/1lb 2oz frozen spinach or 3–4 large bunches fresh spinach)

corn oil

2 tbsp butter

1 large onion

1 clove garlic, crushed

2 sheets pre-rolled puff pastry (25 x 25cm/10 x 10in), rolled out a little thinner

1 egg

salt

175g (6oz) freshly grated parmesan cheese

40g (1½oz) white breadcrumbs

SERVES 6–8

Using your hands, wring out the excess moisture from the spinach, then chop it finely. Heat 1 tablespoon of oil in a frying pan over a medium heat. Drop in the butter and while it is sizzling, add the onion. Cook until lightly golden. Add the garlic, cook for a minute or two, then stir in the spinach. Blend well then take off the heat and leave to cool.

Join the two pastry sheets together on an oiled baking tray (dampen the ends with a little cold water to help them stick). Allow excess pastry to hang over the sides of the tray.

Preheat the oven to 210°C/410°F/gas 6. Mix the egg, ½ teaspoon salt, cheese and breadcrumbs into the cool spinach mixture. If the mixture seems too moist (drops easily off a spoon), add a bit more cheese and a few more breadcrumbs; it should be loose but fall reluctantly from the spoon. Spread over the middle of the pastry, leaving enough room at both ends to fold over and enclose the filling. Bring the ends in to meet the centre and seal them by dampening the edge with a little cold water. Trim to neaten the edges, but ensure the pie is completely sealed. Brush the top lightly with oil, sprinkle generously with salt, then prick lightly with a fork. Put in the oven and bake for 30 minutes, popping any air bubbles that form during baking with a fork. Serve the pie either hot or warm.

Fish, Meat and Poultry

Venetian fish

Sfogi in saor

Based on a Venetian method of cooking and preserving fish, this dish is ideal for entertaining as it is made several hours before serving.

1kg (2¼ lb) smallish white fish fillets, skinned
3 eggs
salt
4 tbsp milk
100ml (3½ fl oz) olive oil
50g (2oz) butter
1 onion, finely sliced or chopped
3 cloves garlic, crushed
40g (1½oz) pine nuts
40g (1½oz) raisins, soaked for 10 minutes in boiling water
1 bay leaf, torn in half
freshly ground black pepper to taste
175ml (6fl oz) white wine vinegar
175ml (6fl oz) cold water
2 tbsp coarsely chopped parsley
75g (3oz) Dried white breadcrumbs (see page 114)
120ml (4fl oz) frying oil

SERVES 8

Rinse the fish fillets and pat them dry with absorbent kitchen paper. Cut each fillet into two or three pieces. Break the eggs into a shallow dish, add a few pinches of salt and beat well with a fork. Beat in the milk, then drop in the pieces of fish. Stir gently to coat, then leave to soak for 30 minutes, stirring occasionally.

Heat the olive oil and butter in a large frying pan over a medium heat. Add the onion and garlic and cook gently, uncovered, until soft and transparent. Add the pine nuts, drained raisins and bay leaf. Grind on some black pepper and cook the mixture for 2–3 minutes. Pour the white wine vinegar in, let it bubble away for a minute, then add the water and ¼ teaspoon of salt. Cook gently for about 10 minutes, then stir in the parsley.

When the marinade is ready, prepare the fish. Tip the breadcrumbs onto a piece of absorbent kitchen paper. Turn the fish into a large colander set over a bowl and drain for 5 minutes. Drop the fish pieces into the breadcrumbs, one at a time, and pat on the crumbs.

When all the fish is prepared, heat most of the frying oil in a large frying pan over a medium-high heat. Drop several pieces of fish in and cook until golden. Turn carefully and cook the other side. Transfer to a large serving platter (don't drain them). Continue frying the fish, adding a little more oil if necessary (watch the heat; lower it a little to stop the crumbs from burning if necessary).

When all the fish fillets are done, spoon the marinade over, ensuring each piece of fish is anointed with some of the liquid. Allow to cool, then cover loosely with a ventilated cover. Leave for several hours before serving.

Fish rolls with pine nuts

Rotolini di pesce con pinoli

Parmesan, breadcrumbs and pine nuts transform fish fillets into irresistible scrumptious mouthfuls. It might pay to double the recipe when you try it...

40g (1½oz) pine nuts
4 tbsp fresh breadcrumbs
4 tbsp freshly grated
  parmesan cheese
¼ teaspoon salt
freshly ground black pepper
  to taste
2 tbsp chopped parsley
3 tbsp melted butter
500g (1lb 2oz) even-sized
  skinned gurnard fillets
  (or other small, firm,
  white fish fillets)
white wine

SERVES 4

Mix the pine nuts, fresh breadcrumbs, parmesan cheese, salt, black pepper, parsley and half of the melted butter in a small bowl.

Remove any skin from the fish fillets, then rinse the fillets and pat them dry with absorbent kitchen paper. Lay them on a clean board, skin side facing up, and cut each one into two or three pieces.

Brush the fish fillets with the rest of the melted butter, then press some of the filling onto each fillet (it tends to fall off, but don't worry – stuff these bits into the tops of the rolls in the next step). Roll up each piece of fish and secure with a toothpick.

Transfer the fish rolls to a shallow, buttered, ovenproof dish, then put in any extra bits of stuffing. Splash with a little white wine and cover with a piece of buttered greaseproof paper or aluminium foil.

Bake in an oven preheated to 180°C/350°F/gas 4 for 5–7 minutes, or until the fish is just starting to cook (changing in colour from opaque to dull white). Remove the paper. Leaving the dish in the oven, turn on the grill, then grill until the topping is golden and the fish is nearly cooked (it will finish cooking with the residual heat). Transfer the fish to a heated serving dish and spoon 2–3 tablespoons of the juices over the top. Serve immediately.

Chicken with lemon and cream

Pollo con limone e panna

This is one of my favourite dishes – the intermittent addition of a little lemon juice or water creates wafts of steam which help keep the chicken moist, but there's not so much liquid that the chicken stews. It develops a rich golden colour and deep flavour without charring: a good Italian trick! The lemon cuts a swathe through the cream so all that remains is its velvety presence.

3 tbsp olive oil
1 small onion, finely chopped
1.3kg (2¾lb) chicken pieces
  (thighs, drumsticks and wings),
  skinned where possible
½ tsp salt
freshly ground black pepper
  to taste
2 tbsp finely chopped rosemary
4 large cloves garlic,
  finely chopped
3 tbsp dry white wine
2 lemons
175ml (6fl oz) single cream

SERVES 6

Put the olive oil in a large non-stick frying pan. Set the pan over a medium heat and add the onion. Cook for 2 minutes, then put the chicken joints in the pan. Cook until golden (about 15 minutes), turning often, and spooning the onion on top of the chicken joints; make sure the heat is not too fierce or the onion will burn.

When the chicken is well browned, sprinkle with salt and black pepper and half the rosemary and garlic. Cook for 1 minute, turning the chicken pieces in the seasonings. Pour the wine in and cook for 3–4 minutes until it has evaporated, then pour the strained juice of 1 lemon over the chicken.

Turn the heat to low and cook gently, adding 2–3 tablespoons of water from time to time to keep the chicken moist until it is tender (it'll take about 45 minutes and about 175ml/6fl oz of water). Sprinkle with the rest of the rosemary and garlic and the strained juice of the second lemon, then mix the cream in.

Cook for a few minutes more or until the creamy juices have thickened slightly (don't over-reduce the juices). Transfer to a hot plate, spoon the juices over and serve immediately. It's not at all traditional to serve a dish like this with noodles – but it's how we've enjoyed it many times in the Biuso household. Cook pasta noodles until al dente, drain and tip into a hot dish. Toss a knob of soft butter through them and serve immediately. Serve a crisp green salad, too.

Poussins with crunchy prosciutto and sage butter

Poussins con prosciutto e salvia

These baby chickens, plump and succulent, wrapped in crispy blankets of prosciutto, emitting nose-teasing wafts of fennel, garlic and sage, are divine.

6 poussins
75g (3oz) butter, melted
½ tsp salt
freshly ground black pepper
   to taste
1½ tsp fennel seeds
4 cloves garlic, crushed
1½ tbsp chopped sage leaves
300g (10oz) thinly
   sliced prosciutto
50ml (2fl oz) dry white wine
herbs for garnishing (small
   bunches of sage, rosemary
   and parsley)

SERVES 6

Rinse the poussins inside and out, removing necks or other matter from cavities. Pat dry. Mix the butter, salt, pepper, fennel seeds, garlic and sage together in a small bowl. Put half a teaspoon of the mixture inside each poussin. Fold the wing tips back then tie the legs and parson's nose together with string on each poussin.

Preheat the oven to 190°C/375°F/gas 5. Brush the poussins generously with the seasoned butter then wrap prosciutto around them (put more on the top than on the underside). Put the poussins in a large roasting dish (there should be space around each poussin so they brown and don't stew) and cook for 35–50 minutes (this depends on the size of the poussins; check juices are clear by piercing the thickest part of a thigh with a skewer, or partially separate one leg from the body of one of the poussins and check that the flesh is cooked).

Brush the poussins with more of the seasoned butter 15 minutes before cooking time is up and again when you take them from the oven. Let them rest for 15 minutes, loosely draped with a piece of aluminium foil, then transfer them to a board and snip off the string.

Pour off any fat from the roasting dish and set the dish over a medium heat and pour in the wine. Bubble up, then distribute the juices between six hot dinner plates. Put a poussin on each plate, garnish with herbs and serve immediately.

Stuffed chicken drumsticks
Coscette di pollo ripiene

The musky scent and spicy flavour of marjoram permeates these chicken legs. A fluffy pillow of potato mash makes a good plate-mate.

120g (4½ oz) thinly sliced
   ham, finely chopped
1 large clove garlic, crushed
1 tbsp chopped marjoram
   (or 1 tsp dried)
2 tbsp finely chopped parsley
4 tbsp freshly grated
   parmesan cheese
1–2 small eggs, lightly beaten
   (I usually use 1 whole egg
   and 1 extra yolk)
salt and freshly ground black
   pepper to taste
12 skinned and boned chicken
   drumsticks (or use chicken
   thighs, trimmed of excess fat)
120ml (4fl oz) olive oil
2 tbsp butter
4 tbsp plain flour mixed with
   ½ tsp salt
120ml (4fl oz) dry white wine
250ml (8fl oz) hot chicken
   stock

SERVES 4–6

In a bowl mix the ham, garlic, herbs and parmesan cheese and blend in enough beaten egg to turn the mixture into a paste. Season with ¼ teaspoon of salt and some black pepper. Smear a little of the stuffing on the inside of each drumstick, then seal by pressing the flesh together.

Heat the olive oil in a large heavy-based frying pan over a medium heat. When it is hot, drop in the butter.

Meanwhile, coat the chicken drumsticks with the seasoned flour, dust off the excess, squeeze them gently to seal the coating, then lower them into the hot pan. Sauté for 15 minutes, turning with tongs halfway through the cooking. Pour off the fat, season them with a little salt and black pepper, then pour the wine over. Let the wine evaporate slowly (for about 10 minutes) and turn the pieces of chicken over once. Start adding the hot stock, a little at a time, pouring a teaspoonful of stock over each drumstick. Continue cooking the chicken pieces for about 15 minutes more or until they are just cooked through. Turn them over from time to time and moisten them with more stock.

When done, transfer the chicken drumsticks to a heated serving dish and pour any juices over the top.

Veal fillet with green olives and fresh bay leaves

Filetto di vitello con olive verdi e alloro

Colourful, tender, tasty, but not cheap! Reserve this for a special dinner.

1kg (2¼ lb) baby new
  potatoes, scrubbed
6 x 150g (5oz) veal loin fillets
1 tbsp olive oil
knob of butter
3 tbsp plain flour
fresh bay leaves
salt
freshly ground black pepper
  to taste
50ml (2fl oz) dry white wine
2 cloves garlic, crushed
175g (6oz) large green
  olives, chopped
pared strips of lemon zest
  from 1 lemon
2 tbsp extra virgin olive oil
1 tbsp chopped marjoram
100g (4oz) cherry tomatoes
1 tbsp torn parsley leaves

SERVES 6

Steam the potatoes until they are just tender. (If the potatoes are not new, just small, peel them first.)

Remove any silvery skin from the veal fillets and pat them dry with absorbent kitchen paper. Choose a large frying pan that has a lid or a large casserole dish (it doesn't have to be deep). Heat the olive oil in the pan or casserole over a medium heat. When it is hot, drop in the butter. Pass the pieces of fillet through the flour and put half of them in the pan (or all of them if they will fit) while the butter is sizzling. Cook on both sides until a good brown colour and transfer them to a plate when done. Repeat with the other pieces of fillet. While the meat is browning, add the bay leaves and let these brown too, covering the pan or casserole with a splatter screen if you have one (the bay leaves tend to spit!). Return all the fillets to the pan, sprinkle with salt, grind on some black pepper and pour the wine in. Immediately cover with the lid, turn the heat to low and cook for about 7 minutes, or until the meat is nearly cooked but still juicy and slightly pink. Turn off the heat and let the meat rest with the lid on for 5 minutes; it will finish cooking by residual heat.

While the meat is cooking, heat the garlic, olives and zest in a pan with the extra virgin olive oil. Cook for 2–3 minutes until hot, then add the potatoes and marjoram. Cook gently, tossing, until piping hot (be careful not to break up the potatoes). Stir the tomatoes and parsley through the potatoes and olives and tip into a serving bowl.

Transfer the meat to a board and reduce the pan juices over a medium heat until they are syrupy. Slice the meat, arrange on a heated plate and pour the juices over. Serve immediately with the potato and olive salad.

Crispy veal with parmesan and black olives

Scaloppine di vitello al parmigiano e olive

Adding parmesan cheese to the breadcrumb crust gives these pieces of veal an appetizing, golden crisp crust and a flavour boost.

500g (1lb 2oz) veal
  scaloppine (see page 13)
75g (3oz) freshly grated
  parmesan cheese
65g (2½oz) Dried white breadcrumbs (see page 114)
salt
2 eggs, beaten with
  a pinch of salt
olive oil
1 tbsp butter
1 large onion, sliced
1 clove garlic, crushed
20 basil leaves
100g (4oz) black olives,
  halved and pitted
freshly ground black pepper
  to taste

SERVES 4

Cut each slice of meat into two or three pieces. Mix the parmesan cheese and breadcrumbs with ¼ teaspoon of salt. Pass the slices of meat through the beaten egg, letting the excess drip off, then coat with the crumb mixture. Put the pieces of veal on a tray in a single layer as they are coated; they can be prepared up to 1 hour before cooking.

Set a large frying pan over a medium heat. When hot, add 2 tablespoons of olive oil and the butter. While the mixture is sizzling, add half the veal pieces to the pan (or as many as will fit without overlapping) and cook until golden brown on both sides (take care not to let them burn). Transfer the cooked veal to a heated plate and keep it warm while cooking the rest of the meat; add more oil and butter if necessary.

Meanwhile, put the onion and garlic and 2 tablespoons of olive oil in a small frying pan, set it over a gentle heat, and cook until soft and lightly golden. Add the basil leaves and olives, grind on some black pepper and heat through for 1 minute.

Arrange the veal on a heated serving plate and spoon the olive garnish down the centre. Serve immediately.

Roasted eye fillet wrapped in pancetta
Filetto di bue con pancetta

I don't think I need to say anything about this dish – the picture says it all. Yum!

1kg (2¼ lb) fillet of beef,
  cut from the thick end
1 tbsp chopped rosemary
2 tbsp olive oil
1 clove garlic, crushed
1 tsp salt
½ tsp freshly ground
  black pepper
200g (7oz) thinly sliced
  pancetta (or prosciutto)

SERVES 6

Preheat the oven to 210°C/410°F/gas 6. Remove any fat and silver-skin from the beef. Mix the rosemary, 1 tablespoon of the olive oil, the garlic, salt and black pepper together in a shallow dish. Roll the beef in the mixture then wrap it in pancetta and tie it on with string as best you can.

Heat the remaining tablespoon of olive oil in a roasting tin over a high heat and carefully lower the beef in. Turn the beef quickly in the hot oil then put it in the oven and cook for 15 minutes for rare to medium-rare, or until it is done to your liking. Take the beef out of the oven and let it rest for 10–15 minutes.

Remove the string from the beef. Put absorbent kitchen paper around the edges of the chopping board to absorb the juices. Slice the meat into thick, even slices. Rest the sliced meat for 1 minute, mop up the juices, then transfer to the plate and serve immediately.

Lamb abruzzi   Agnello all'abruzzese

I've cooked hundreds of lamb dishes over the years, but this one is tops. It's succulent and tender, and you'll be hard pushed not to pick at bits of the crisp parmesan coating. Reserve balsamico tradizionale for special dishes; a balsamic aged up to five years will be sufficient here.

3 tbsp finely chopped
   streaky bacon
3 cloves garlic, crushed
1 tbsp finely chopped
   rosemary
2 tbsp finely chopped parsley
freshly ground black pepper
1.5–2kg (3–4½lb) leg of lamb,
   trimmed of excess fat
2 tbsp olive oil
120ml (4fl oz) balsamic
   vinegar (or red wine vinegar)
1 tsp salt
2 tbsp freshly grated
   parmesan cheese
3 tbsp fresh white breadcrumbs
2 tbsp soft butter

SERVES 6

Preheat the oven to 190°C/375°F/gas 5. Mix the bacon, garlic, rosemary, parsley and a little black pepper in a small bowl. Make a dozen or so deep incisions in the meaty parts of the lamb and force the stuffing into these slits, using the end of a teaspoon.

Put the olive oil in a roasting tin and put in the oven. When the oil is hot, add the lamb, coating it in the hot oil to seal. Grind over some black pepper and roast the meat for 45 minutes, basting occasionally. Pour the balsamic vinegar over, sprinkle with the salt and return to the oven for a further 15 minutes.

Meanwhile, mix together the parmesan cheese, breadcrumbs and butter. Spread this over the top of the lamb and return it to the oven for another 15 minutes. Remove the lamb from the oven and let it rest at room temperature, covered loosely with aluminium foil (poke a few holes in the foil so the lamb doesn't steam), for 15 minutes before slicing. (This produces a moist pink roast but, if you prefer the lamb a little more cooked, allow an extra 10–15 minutes in the initial cooking stage.)

Transfer the lamb to a chopping board. Tilt the roasting tin, scoop off and discard the fat, then bubble up the juices over a medium heat for a minute or two. Slice the lamb thinly, arrange it on a serving plate, pour the pan juices over and serve immediately.

Leg of lamb with parmesan crust and crunchy potatoes

Coscia di agnello e patate arrosto

This dish is a less complex version of Lamb abruzzi (see page 81), with the addition of potatoes, which cook until crusty around the lamb. Omitting the bacon from the lamb makes it less gamey. A good family roast.

1 leg of lamb, partially boned, weighing approximately 1.8kg (4½ lb) (ask the butcher to remove the aitchbone, leaving the shank bone in)
3 cloves garlic, sliced
rosemary sprigs
120ml (4fl oz) white wine
1.5kg (3lb) roasting potatoes (starchy ones), peeled and cut into large chunks
olive oil
salt
3 tbsp fresh breadcrumbs
50g (2oz) freshly grated parmesan cheese
freshly ground black pepper to taste
3 tbsp soft butter

SERVES 6–8

Preheat the oven to 180°C/350°F/gas 4. Trim as much fat as possible from the lamb. Stud the lamb with slivers of garlic and sprigs of rosemary. Put it in a roasting tin and set this over a medium element. Heat for 3–4 minutes until it starts to sizzle, then pour the wine over.

Meanwhile, rub the potatoes with olive oil and salt and set these around the lamb; the tin should be crowded. Roast the meat and potatoes in the oven for 1 hour, basting and turning the potatoes from time to time.

In a small bowl mix the breadcrumbs, parmesan cheese, black pepper to taste, ½ teaspoon of salt and the butter. Remove the lamb from the oven and spread this over the top. Return the lamb to the oven and cook for a further 10–15 minutes, or until it is done to your liking (this should produce pink, juicy lamb with a good crust on top).

Transfer the lamb to a board and let it rest for 15 minutes. Continue cooking the potatoes while the lamb rests. Slice the lamb into thin pieces and arrange on a heated serving platter. Serve the potatoes separately. Accompany with a green salad.

Sausage coil with hot polenta and sautéed mushrooms

Salsiccia con polenta e funghi saltati

Keeping sausage meat in an uninterrupted loop, twirling it into a coil and securing it with wooden skewers is a trick I learned from my Italian mother-in-law, Rosa. You will need to order the sausage from a sausage-maker (many butchers make their own sausages). Just tell them to give you an unbroken length of sausage, preferably a thinner sausage, about 2–3 metres (6½–9¾ feet) long. Make sure you use a good-quality flavoursome sausage, not the sawdust kind!

½ quantity Basic polenta (see page 121)
3m (9¾ft) length of sausage
75g (3oz) butter
500g (1lb 2oz) button mushrooms,
  thickly sliced
2 large cloves garlic, crushed
freshly ground black pepper to taste
½ tsp salt
2 tbsp coarsely chopped parsley
1 tsp finely chopped rosemary

SERVES 6

Soak a few wooden skewers in cold water for 15–20 minutes.

Make the polenta first and, while it is cooking, cook the sausage and mushroom sauce. (This will keep you busy but, providing everything is prepared, it can be done. Alternatively, the mushrooms can be cooked ahead, cooled, then reheated in the microwave – and you can opt for quick-cooking polenta.)

Curl the sausage into a large, preferably non-stick, frying pan. Secure the sausage coil with three or four skewers, pushing the skewers right through the flat coil of sausage from one side to the other.

Set the cold pan over a medium-high heat (you shouldn't need any oil) and cook until the sausage is lightly browned underneath. Turn it over and cook the second side until it is lightly browned, then lower the heat and cook gently, turning once more, until it is cooked through (if any liquid accumulates, pour it off). Remove the sausage from the pan, pull out the skewers and drain briefly on absorbent kitchen paper.

While the sausage is cooking and while you intermittently stir the polenta, sauté the mushrooms. Heat a large frying pan over a medium heat, then drop two-thirds of the butter in. When it is sizzling, increase the heat to medium-high and drop the mushrooms in. Toss them in the butter, then cook,

stirring often, until any liquid evaporates and the mushrooms are starting to brown.

Stir the garlic through, grind on some black pepper and continue cooking until the garlic is lightly browned. Sprinkle with the salt and add the herbs. Turn off the heat.

Now co-ordinate the meal. To finish off, turn the hot polenta into a heated serving bowl and top with the sausage coil. Quickly reheat the mushrooms over a high heat and add the last of the butter. As soon as it melts, pour the contents of the pan over the sausage and polenta. Serve immediately.

Pork chops with fennel and rosemary

Costolette di maiale con semi di finocchio e rosmarino

The tantalizing fragrance of plump pork cutlets, rosemary, fennel seeds and garlic as they are singed by the flames of the barbecue is enough to bring the neighbours over!

1 stalk of rosemary
6 tbsp extra virgin olive oil
1½ tsp fennel seeds
16 fresh bay leaves
freshly ground black pepper
8 large cloves garlic, chopped
8 large pork chops or cutlets
salt

SERVES 6–8

Remove spikes from the rosemary, chop roughly and put in a large shallow container with the olive oil, fennel seeds, bay leaves, black pepper and garlic. Mix together with a fork then put in the chops or cutlets. Spread the mixture over the meat, cover with plastic food wrap and chill for several hours, turning the chops occasionally. Bring to room temperature before cooking.

Cook for 2–3 minutes a side on a hot barbecue plate, anoint with more of the marinade, then finish off over the barbecue grill rack. The flames should leap and lick the chops, singeing the outside and impregnating them with smoke. Cook for 2–3 minutes over the flaring grill then transfer to a serving plate. Sprinkle generously with salt then leave the chops to settle for 10 minutes before serving.

Tuscan pork and beans

Maiale con fagioli alla Toscana

Pork and beans – perfect winter rib-sticking stuff!

225g (8oz) cannellini beans (if not available, use white beans of your choice but be aware that they may take longer to cook), rinsed, soaked overnight in cold water and drained

3 tbsp extra virgin olive oil

1 small onion, finely chopped

½ carrot, finely chopped

1 small stick celery (choose an inner stalk), finely chopped

300g (10oz) pork spare ribs (buy them "in the piece", not cut into individual ribs, cut from the short end)

2 fresh bay leaves

1 tsp finely chopped rosemary

1 tbsp coarsely chopped flat leaf parsley

freshly ground black pepper to taste

200g (7oz) canned Italian tomatoes, well mashed

1½ tsp salt

SERVES 6

Put the beans in a saucepan and cover generously with water. Bring to the boil, removing any scum as it rises. Lower the heat and cover with a lid (set the temperature so that the liquid is boiling gently without boiling over – the beans will cook more quickly like this). Cook for 30–40 minutes, or until nicely tender. Drain, reserving the liquid. Cover the beans with a piece of absorbent kitchen paper until required.

Put the extra virgin olive oil in a medium-sized saucepan with the onion and set the pan over a medium heat. Cook gently until lightly coloured. Add the carrot, celery, pork ribs, bay leaves, rosemary and parsley. Grind on plenty of black pepper. Cook for 10 minutes, stirring often.

Stir in the tomatoes and beans and 1 litre (1¾ pints) of the bean cooking water (make up to 1 litre/1¾ pints with water if necessary). Bring to the boil. Lower the heat and cook, uncovered, for 30 minutes. Stir in the salt, then mash some of the beans with a potato masher to thicken the soup. Dish into soup bowls and serve hot.

Vegetables and Salads

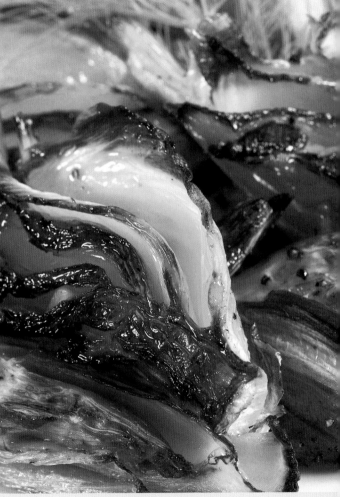

Crunchy potato sticks

Patate croccanti

A potato is just a potato until you add something naughty – in this case olive oil and butter – with which you can turn them into utterly irresistible, deep golden, crunchy morsels. You'll be surprised by how a bowl of these can bring out porcine characters in your dining companions.

2kg (4½ lb) roasting
    potatoes, peeled
3 tbsp olive oil
2 tbsp butter
1 tsp salt or to taste
2 tbsp finely
    chopped rosemary

SERVES 6

Preheat the oven to 180°C/350°F/gas 4. Cut the potatoes into rough chunks and dry on absorbent kitchen paper. Put them in a roasting tin, drizzle with olive oil and dot with butter. Sprinkle the salt and the rosemary over the top.

Cook the potatoes in the oven, turning occasionally with a fish slice, for 1¼ hours or until they are crisp and golden.

Baby potatoes on rosemary stalks
Spiedini di patate al rosmarino

Skewering baby potatoes on rosemary stalks gives them a wonderfully resinous, rosemary fragrance. Finishing them over the barbecue grill imparts a whiff of smokiness. The potatoes must be waxy ones (sometimes sold as "salad potatoes") to ensure they will hold together on the skewers (starchy potatoes will fall off). Choose firm, woody stalks of rosemary. If you're buying the herb, it's a good idea to dry the stalks for a day or two before using them.

1kg (2¼ lb) freshly dug small
   potatoes, scrubbed
3 small dried "bird's eye"
   chillies, crushed
4 tbsp extra virgin olive oil
½ tsp salt
12 long, firm stalks of
   rosemary

SERVES 4–6

Cook the potatoes until they are nearly tender (preferably steam them; alternatively, cook them gently in water). When the potatoes are cool, cut them in half. Put the chillies, extra virgin olive oil and salt in a shallow rectangular dish. Thread the potato chunks onto the rosemary stalks. If this is difficult to do, carefully make holes with a fine skewer first. Gently brush the potatoes with the flavoured oil.

Cook them on a hot barbecue plate until they are golden, anointing them with the oil marinade during cooking. Serve hot.

Potatoes with rosemary

Patate con rosmarino

Italians may be known for being pasta experts, but they're pretty good with hot oil and a frying pan too. The vinegar added at the end gives a tantalizing fragrance and flavour, but it does soften the potatoes; omit it if you want to keep the potatoes crunchy.

1kg (2¼ lb) roasting potatoes,
   peeled and cubed
120ml (4fl oz) olive oil
6 large cloves garlic,
   very finely chopped
1 tbsp finely chopped
   rosemary
½ tsp salt
freshly ground black pepper
   to taste
50ml (2fl oz) white wine
   vinegar

SERVES 4–6

Turn the potato cubes onto a clean tea towel or absorbent kitchen paper and pat dry.

Put the olive oil in a large heavy-based frying pan and heat over a medium-high heat. Add the potato cubes, toss in the oil and cook for 2–3 minutes. Cover with a lid (leaving it slightly ajar for steam to escape), turn to low and cook very gently for 1 hour, turning the potato cubes often until they are crisp. Watch the heat; if it is too high, the potatoes will form a hard, glazed surface on the outside, yet remain uncooked on the inside.

Remove the lid, increase the heat to medium and add the garlic and rosemary. Sprinkle with the salt and grind on some black pepper. Cook for 3–4 minutes or until the garlic takes on a little colour. Pour the white wine vinegar over the potatoes and toss well. Cook for 2–3 minutes more, then tip all the contents of the pan into a hot serving dish and serve immediately.

Barbecued radicchio

Radicchio alla griglia

Barbecuing radicchio is not as silly as it sounds, providing you strip back the bitter, strong-tasting outer leaves and barbecue it over a gentle heat. The radicchio will retain some of its bitter-ness, but this is part of its character. The other ingredients add tiers of complexity to the chargrilled radicchio. Use the best extra virgin olive oil and balsamic vinegar you can afford. I think radicchio cooked like this tastes like artichokes.

40g (1½oz) pine nuts
4 balls radicchio, trimmed and
    outer bitter leaves removed
2 tbsp extra virgin olive oil
1 tbsp fresh marjoram leaves
¼ tsp salt
freshly ground black pepper
    to taste
1 tbsp balsamic vinegar

SERVES 4–6

Toast the pine nuts in a small, dry pan or fry them in a little hot oil. (I prefer to fry them in oil).

Cut the balls of radicchio in half or into quarters if large. Mix the extra virgin olive oil in a large bowl with the marjoram, salt and black pepper and put in the radicchio. Toss well. Cook gently, on a barbecue plate that has just been heated, until the radicchio is lightly browned – watch the heat doesn't get too fierce or the radicchio will burn and the bitter flavour, which is pleasant in a small dose, will become too much.

Turn onto a plate and drizzle with balsamic vinegar and a little extra oil. Season with extra salt and black pepper, toss well, scatter the pine nuts over and serve hot or hottish.

"Smothered" cauliflower

Cavolfiore affogato

"Smothering" cauliflower in wine, pine nuts, raisins, chillies and parsley certainly livens it up.

50ml (2fl oz) olive oil
2 large cloves garlic, peeled and lightly crushed
1 medium cauliflower, cut into florets
¼ tsp salt
freshly ground black pepper to taste
120ml (4fl oz) dry white wine
2 tbsp pine nuts
1½ tbsp raisins
3 tiny dried "bird's eye" chillies, crushed (optional)
1 tbsp finely chopped parsley

SERVES 6

Heat the olive oil in a large frying pan over a low heat. Add the garlic cloves and fry gently until golden brown, remove and discard.

Add the cauliflower, toss in the oil, cover the pan with a lid and cook for 5 minutes, shaking the pan occasionally. Add salt and black pepper. Pour in the wine and stir through the nuts and raisins. Put the lid back on, bring to the boil, then lower the heat and simmer for 10–15 minutes.

Remove the lid and allow the liquid to evaporate until syrupy. Stir through the crushed chillies and parsley. Allow to cool before serving.

Charred courgettes with pesto

Zucchine alla griglia con pesto

This dish is great as an accompaniment to barbecued meats or as part of an all-vegetable barbecue.

6–8 firm smallish courgettes, green or yellow
1 tbsp extra virgin olive oil
salt
freshly ground black pepper
2 tbsp pesto, preferably homemade
   (see page 117)

SERVES 6

Trim the courgettes, cut them in half lengthwise, then score the cut surfaces with a sharp knife. Put them in a large bowl and drizzle with the oil. Sprinkle on a little salt, grind on some pepper, then rub the oil and seasonings all over the courgettes.

Cook them on a hot barbecue plate until lightly charred. If the pesto is stiff, thin it with a little warm water. Spread it over the cut surfaces of the courgettes then stack them on a plate. Serve at room temperature.

Baby peas with sautéed prosciutto

Pisellini con prosciutto

If fresh peas are not available, substitute frozen baby peas.

2 tbsp olive oil
1 clove garlic, finely chopped
75g (3oz) prosciutto or ham, diced
freshly ground black pepper to taste
¼ tsp salt
1kg (2¼lb) fresh peas, shelled, or use
   300g (10oz) frozen baby peas
2 tbsp finely chopped parsley

SERVES 4

Put the olive oil and garlic in a small saucepan and set over a medium heat. Cook until the garlic is a light nut-brown colour. Add the prosciutto or ham and cook briefly, stirring. Grind on some black pepper, add the salt and peas and pour in 50ml (2fl oz) of water. Cover with a lid and cook for about 15 minutes. (If using frozen peas, cook them with 3 tablespoons of water for about 5 minutes before adding them to the pan.)

Check the seasoning and stir in the parsley. Transfer to a bowl and serve.

Withered carrots

Carote con parmigiano

The savoury flavours of these carrots go with many dishes. Don't be tempted to serve them crunchy – you'll be missing the point.

900g (2lb) carrots, peeled and thinly sliced
2 knobs butter
¼ tsp salt
freshly ground black pepper to taste
2 tbsp chopped Italian parsley
4 tbsp freshly grated parmesan cheese

SERVES 6

Put the carrots in a large, heavy-based frying pan and dot with the butter. Pour on 120ml (4fl oz) water and add the salt.

Bring to the boil, lower the heat to medium-low and let the water evaporate. Add another 50ml (2fl oz) of water and continue cooking, stirring often. Add another 50ml (2fl oz) of water and continue cooking until it evaporates. If the carrots are not tender, add another 50ml (2fl oz) of water and continue cooking, adding more water if necessary, until they are tender.

Grind on a little black pepper then transfer the carrots to a heated serving bowl. Sprinkle on the parsley and parmesan, toss and serve immediately.

Fennel, sweet tomato and olive salad

Insalata di finocchi, pomodori e olive

Crisp crunch and colour are the hallmarks of this superb salad. If you can, choose a gutsy, fruity olive oil to complement the sweet fruit taste of the tomatoes and the fresh anise flavour of the fennel.

2 fennel bulbs
  (if the fennel is slim,
  increase the quantity to 4)
150g (5oz) sweet cherry
  tomatoes, halved
50g (2oz) black olives
1 tsp lemon juice
½ tsp salt
freshly ground black pepper
  to taste
2 tbsp coarsely chopped
  parsley
3 tbsp extra virgin olive oil

SERVES 6–8

Prepare the fennel by trimming away the root end and removing stems and bruised parts. Slice into thinnish strips and put in a bowl with the cherry tomatoes and olives.

Whisk the lemon juice, salt, black pepper and parsley together in a small bowl, then blend in the extra virgin olive oil. Pour over the salad, toss well and serve.

Roasted fennel

Finocchi al forno

Serve this dish with grilled or barbecued fish, rabbit or chicken, or use in a risotto. Accompany with segments of lemon to squeeze over.

3–4 medium fennel bulbs
extra virgin olive oil
freshly ground black pepper to taste
lemon segments

SERVES 4–6

Preheat the oven to 200°C/400°F/ gas 6. Trim the fennel bulbs then cut them into quarters through the root. Rub them generously with extra virgin olive oil, put them in a shallow-sided ovenproof dish and grind on some black pepper. Cook the fennel in the oven for 20–30 minutes, or until it is tender and lightly browned, turning once.

Salad of red leaves with caper dressing

Insalata di foglioline e capperi

Some kind of indefinable magic is created by teaming bitter radicchio leaves with the sea-tang of capers, the pungency of garlic, the fruitiness of extra virgin olive oil and the sweet piquancy of parmesan cheese. Perhaps the best salad I've ever eaten.

1 tbsp white wine vinegar
1 tbsp capers, drained
1 clove garlic, crushed
1 tbsp coarsely chopped parsley
120ml (4fl oz) extra virgin olive oil
50g (2oz) freshly grated parmesan cheese
3–6 balls of radicchio (use 3 large or 6 small ones)

SERVES 4–6

Blend the vinegar, capers, garlic and parsley together in a food processor fitted with the chopping blade. While the machine is running, dribble in the olive oil, then stop the machine, scatter the cheese over and process briefly until it is blended. Alternatively, make by hand – blend all the ingredients, except the oil, in a bowl with a fork. Slowly mix in the oil.

Tear the radicchio into bite-sized pieces and place in a salad bowl. Pour the dressing over, toss well, then serve.

Right *Roasted fennel*

Desserts

Lemon ricotta flan

Torta di ricotta al limone

This tangy-sweet flan is a favourite with those who don't have an excessively sweet tooth. It seems to have just the right balance of creaminess, sweetness and lemony tang.

1 quantity Rich shortcrust
  pastry (see page 122)
300g (10oz) ricotta cheese
150g (5oz) caster sugar
grated zest of 2 lemons
3 eggs, at room temperature
50ml (2fl oz) strained
  lemon juice
icing sugar for dusting

SERVES 8

Make the pastry and line a 23cm (9in) flan ring with it. Chill for 30 minutes, then bake blind for 10 minutes (see page 123).

The filling is quickly made in a food processor. Alternatively, use a hand-held electric beater. Process the ricotta cheese to break it up, then, with the machine running, pour in the caster sugar. Process until it is well blended, then add the lemon zest. With the machine running, drop in the eggs one at a time and process until they are amalgamated, scraping the sides of the bowl if necessary. Blend in the lemon juice.

Preheat the oven to 200°C/400°F/gas 6. Pour the mixture into the pastry case, then transfer the flan to the oven. Bake for 15 minutes, then lower the heat to 170°C/325°F/gas 3 and bake for 15–20 minutes more, or until the custard is just set and lightly golden.

Slide the flan onto a cake rack to cool. Before serving, sift icing sugar over the top. This tart is best eaten the day it is made.

Peaches stuffed with amaretti

Pesche ripiene con amaretti

If you have difficulty extracting the peach stones, cut them out with a serrated grapefruit knife. Cut off any flesh adhering to the stones, chop finely and add to the amaretti mixture in the bowl.

75g (3oz) coarsely crushed
  amaretti biscuits
50g (2oz) caster sugar
4 tbsp cocoa powder
100ml (3½ fl oz) fruity, dry
  white wine
6 medium or 12 small peaches
  or nectarines, ripe but firm
butter

Mascarpone cream
300g (10oz) mascarpone
120ml (4fl oz) single cream
caster sugar to taste

SERVES 6

Preheat the oven to 180°C/350°F/gas 4. Put the crushed amaretti biscuits in a bowl with the caster sugar. Sieve the cocoa powder over, then add 2 tablespoons of the wine and mix.

Cut the peaches in half through their natural indentations, twist, then pull apart and extract the stones. Put the peaches in a shallow baking dish, cut side up. Put a teaspoonful of the amaretti mixture in the cavity of each peach, then top with a small pat of butter. Pour the remaining wine over the top. Bake in the oven for 30 minutes or until the fruit is tender.

Meanwhile, gently mix together the mascarpone cream ingredients in a bowl, then mound in soft peaks on individual plates. Arrange the baked peaches on the plates and pour any juices over the cream. Alternatively, top each peach with a dollop of cream and a spoonful of crushed amaretti. Serve immediately. These are best eaten the day they are made.

Crumbly almond cake

Torta di mandorle friabile

Not that I'm one to name-drop, but when I served this cake to the Marchese de Frescobaldi (head of the Frescobaldi Wine Estate in Tuscany) he said it was as good as any he had eaten in Tuscany. Try it with a drop of Frescobaldi's Vin Santo. If you don't have a food processor, chop or grind the almonds finely, then mix everything together in a large bowl.

120g (4½oz) unblanched almonds
120g (4½oz) plain flour
120g (4½oz) granulated sugar
90g (3½oz) finely ground corn meal
grated zest of 1 lemon
120g (4½oz) butter, softened
2 egg yolks, at room temperature
icing sugar for dusting
Vin Santo for serving

SERVES AT LEAST 8

Preheat the oven to 180°C/350°F/gas 4. Put the almonds in a small saucepan, cover with water, bring to the boil, then cool and flick off the skins. Transfer the almonds to a shallow ovenproof dish and toast them in the oven until they are a pale brown colour. Cool, then chop in a food processor. Stop the machine and tip in the flour, granulated sugar and corn meal. Blend, then sprinkle the lemon zest on and drop in the butter and egg yolks. Process until it is well mixed and crumbly.

Butter a shallow 23cm (9in) round ovenproof dish (or sandwich tin) and line with a disk of baking parchment, then press the mixture into the tin. Dust with icing sugar and bake in the oven for 35–40 minutes. If the cake starts to brown too quickly, lower the heat. Mark into small wedges while still warm. When cool, store in an airtight container. Just before serving splash with a little Vin Santo or serve the Vin Santo separately, in small glasses.

Lattice topped rice puddings

Budino di riso

These puddings are best eaten at room temperature, but they can be cooled, refrigerated and served the day after they are made.

30g (1oz) (approximately 4) dried apricots
165g (5½oz) Italian rice – arborio, vialone nano, carnaroli
500ml (18fl oz) milk
120g (4½oz) caster sugar
¼ tsp ground cinnamon
grated zest of 1 lemon
75g (3oz) unsalted butter, plus extra for greasing the moulds
3 egg yolks
icing sugar for dusting

SERVES 6

Put the apricots in a bowl, cover with hot water and soak them for several hours (or until tender). Drain, then chop roughly.

Bring 1 litre (1¾ pints) of water to the boil, tip in the rice and cook at a gentle boil for 5 minutes. Drain. Rinse the pan and put in the milk and sugar. Stir until the sugar dissolves, then return the rice to the pan and add the cinnamon and zest. Cook over a low heat for 15 minutes, stirring often, (the mixture should be creamy). Stir in the butter, then mix in the apricots and egg yolks.

Preheat the oven to 170°C/325°F/gas 3. Spoon into six buttered moulds or ramekins. Sit them inside a shallow baking dish and bake for 30 minutes or until they are lightly golden on top. Allow to cool, then unmould them. Sieve a little icing sugar over the top.

Heat a metal skewer over a gas flame or an electric element until it is very hot (be sure to wear an oven glove) then, using the hot end, mark out a lattice pattern on the top of the puddings; reheat the skewer as necessary.

Pine nut torte

Pinolata

Rich and almondy, with a crown of golden pine nuts, this torte is always greedily devoured.

1 quantity Rich shortcrust
   pastry (see page 122)
120g (4½oz) butter, softened
175g (6oz) caster sugar
3 tbsp plain flour
2 eggs plus 2 egg yolks,
   lightly beaten together
175g (6oz) ground almonds
165g (5½oz) pine nuts
6 tbsp apricot jam or
   apricot conserve
cream for serving

SERVES 8–10

Make the pastry and line a 25cm (9¾in) flan ring with it (there will be some left over). Chill for 30 minutes, then bake "blind" for 10 minutes (see page 123).

Put the butter in a warmed bowl and beat with an electric mixer until it is light and creamy. Beat in the caster sugar by degrees and continue beating until the mixture is well creamed. Sprinkle the flour over, then, with the machine running, beat in the eggs and egg yolks by degrees (this can be done in a food processor). Fold in the almonds and 50g (2oz) of the pine nuts.

Preheat the oven to 180°C/350°F/gas 4. Spread the apricot jam or conserve over the pastry case, then put in the almond filling. Smooth the surface with a knife and sprinkle the rest of the pine nuts over the top.

Bake for about 40 minutes or until the pastry is browned and crisp on the base (drape a piece of aluminium foil over the top of the pie to deflect top heat once the pastry has coloured). Cool for 5 minutes, then remove the flan ring and transfer the tart to a cooling rack. Serve at room temperature with cream.

Honeymoon cake

Torta di luna miele

I don't know how this cake got its name, but you don't have to be on your honeymoon to enjoy it!

melted butter, caster sugar and
   plain flour to prepare the tin
100g (4oz) butter
3 medium, tart cooking apples
juice and zest of 1 lemon
4 eggs
120g (4½oz) caster sugar
150g (5oz) plain flour
pinch of salt
1 level tsp baking powder
icing sugar for dusting

SERVES AT LEAST 8

Prepare the tin first according to the instructions opposite. Preheat the oven to 180°C/350°F/gas 4.

Melt the butter gently, then set aside to cool. Peel and core the apples, then slice them thinly. Put the apples in a large bowl and squeeze the juice of the lemon over. Toss well.

Break the eggs into the bowl of a large food mixer (or food processor). Beat with the whisk until they are blended, then pour the caster sugar in slowly. Continue beating until the mixture leaves a thick trail off the up-held beaters (this may take up to 5 minutes). Sprinkle the lemon zest over and transfer to a large bowl.

Sift the flour, salt and baking powder together on to a piece of paper, then sift half of it over the egg mixture. Fold in lightly with a large spoon. Pour the cooled, melted butter around the sides of the bowl, then fold in until it is only just amalgamated. Sieve the rest of the dry ingredients over and fold in. Drain off any juice from the sliced apples, then very carefully fold the apples into the sponge mixture.

Transfer the mixture to the prepared tin. Smooth the surface lightly with a knife and place in the oven. Bake for about 40 minutes or until the cake is firm but springy to the touch, a rich golden colour and is pulling away slightly from the sides of the tin. Remove from the oven and rest it for 10 minutes. Invert onto a cooling rack and leave the cake to cool completely. Sift icing sugar over before slicing the cake into wedges.

Cake tin preparation

Choose a 23cm (9in) diameter cake tin. Cut a disk of non-stick baking parchment for the base and a strip to go around the sides. Fold the long edge of the strip over by 5cm (2in), then nick the edges of the parchment with scissors. Brush one side of the parchment with melted butter, then sprinkle it generously with caster sugar. Tap off the excess.

Dust the parchment with flour, then tap off the excess. Put the strip of parchment, sugared side facing inwards, around the sides of the tin, so that the folded edge sits flat, then fit the circle of parchment in the centre (this should sit on top of the folded-over, "nicked" edge of the strip of parchment, holding everything in place). This will ensure that the cake does not stick.

Hazelnut and amaretti cupola

Cupola di nocciole e amaretti

Homemade ice cream always brings praise but, when it is chock-full of hazelnuts and crushed amaretti biscuits and served with peaches and strawberries in a sweet honeyed wine, don't be surprised if you catch your guests licking their plates!

100g (4oz) hazelnuts
300ml (½ pt) double cream
½ vanilla pod
40g (1½oz) icing sugar
4 eggs
10 amaretti biscuits,
   partially crushed
6 large ripe peaches
lemon juice
2 tbsp caster sugar
50ml (2fl oz) dessert wine
675g (1½lb) strawberries,
   hulled, sliced if large

SERVES 6–8

Preheat the oven to 180°C/350°F/gas 4. Put the hazelnuts in a shallow ovenproof dish and toast in the oven for about 10 minutes or until a golden colour is visible through the burst skins. Rub vigorously in a clean cloth to remove skins. Coarsely chop.

Choose a bowl with a 1.25–1.5 litre (2¼–2½ pint) capacity and line it with aluminium foil. Put the cream in another bowl, split the vanilla pod lengthwise and scrape the seeds into the cream. Whip with an electric or rotary beater. As the cream starts to thicken, add the icing sugar and beat until it is stiff.

Separate the eggs, placing the yolks in the bowl with the cream, and the egg whites in a grease-free bowl. Blend the egg yolks through the cream with the amaretti biscuits and 75g (3oz) of toasted hazelnuts. Whisk the egg whites until they are stiff, then carefully fold them through the cream mixture with a large spoon. Spoon into the prepared foil-lined bowl and freeze. Once frozen, cover the top of the bowl with aluminium foil to avoid contamination and unwanted odours (don't cover it before it's frozen as the foil will stick to the ice cream). The dessert can be stored frozen for several days.

Plunge the peaches for 20 seconds into a saucepan of boiling water sharpened with a tablespoon of lemon juice. Lift out and plunge into a bowl of cold water. Peel and cut into halves or slices. Put the caster sugar and wine in a bowl and stir until the sugar dissolves. Add the strawberries and peaches to the bowl (best done no longer than 1 hour before serving).

Turn the frozen "cupola" onto a large plate and peel off the aluminium foil. Spoon the fruit around the sides and drizzle the top and sides with the juices. Scatter the remaining hazelnuts over the top and serve immediately.

Basics

Dried white breadcrumbs

Dried white breadcrumbs are used primarily for coating foods that are to be fried. Usually, the items for frying are floured and dipped in beaten egg, which makes a sticky base to which the crumbs adhere. The protein in the egg coagulates when the food is immersed in the fat and this makes an impenetrable wall. For this reason "egging and crumbing" should be done with great care because if it is patchy the fat will enter the food, making it greasy. Dried white breadcrumbs are used to thicken this protective wall and to give the food a crisp, crunchy exterior, which is also appealing to the eye. Fresh white breadcrumbs should not be used as they contain moisture – this will cause the fat to spit and the crumbs may not adhere. Dried, browned breadcrumbs (available commercially) are unsuitable for frying as they will be over-browned before the food is cooked through.

To make dried breadcrumbs, spread a batch of fresh white breadcrumbs in a baking dish and bake in a low oven (120°C/250°F/gas ½) until crisp and dry, but not coloured. Turn them from time to time to ensure they dry evenly. They may take as long as 45 minutes, but don't be tempted to increase the heat. When they are very dry, take them out of the oven and push them through a metal sieve, or blend them in a food processor or liquidiser again until a fine crumb is achieved. If they feel at all moist, return them to the baking dish and continue drying in the oven. When completely cool, store in an airtight container. Dried breadcrumbs will last for many months.

Oven-baked aubergine

Fried aubergine is rich and delicious, but it has a bad habit of soaking up too much oil. If the aubergine is to be incorporated into other dishes (e.g. Aubergine pie page 52, Oven-baked aubergine risotto page 56), it can be brushed with olive oil and oven-baked. This uses much less oil than frying and ensures the dish it is incorporated into does not become excessively rich and oily.

Preheat the oven to 180°C/350°F/gas 4. Slice the aubergines into rounds and brush both sides with olive oil. Lay the slices flat in one layer on a baking tray (line the tray with a teflon baking sheet if you have one). Bake for 20 minutes, or until tender and brown. Use immediately, or cool, refrigerate and use within 24 hours.

Fish stock

Fish bones are high in gelatine so when making fish stock the proportion of bones to water is low. Cook the stock for 20 minutes only; long cooking can make the stock bitter. The vegetables should be cut into small pieces so the flavour can be extracted.

1 fish frame, rinsed (you may need to order this
    from the fishmonger)
peeled rind of 1 small lemon
1 onion, sliced
1 carrot, sliced
1 bay leaf
blade of mace
a few peppercorns
2.25L (4pt) cold water

MAKES 2 LITRES (3½ PINTS)

Put all the ingredients in a saucepan. Bring to the boil, then lower the heat and simmer for 20 minutes. Strain immediately. Refrigerate when cool. Use within 24 hours or freeze for up to 4 weeks.

Chunky tomato sauce

This is a good, all-purpose tomato sauce which can be used in a variety of vegetable dishes, or served alongside them. It is a great sauce for pasta and is best with fat pasta tubes.

2 tbsp olive oil
1 smallish onion, finely chopped
2 cloves garlic, finely chopped
2 x 400g (14oz) cans Italian tomatoes, mashed
1 tbsp tomato purée
1 tsp sugar
¼ tsp salt
freshly ground black pepper to taste

MAKES 500ML (18FL OZ)

Put the olive oil in a saucepan, set over a medium heat and add the onion. Cook for 2–3 minutes, stirring occasionally, then add the garlic. Cover, lower the heat and cook gently until soft.

Add the tomatoes, stir well, then mix in the tomato purée, sugar, salt and black pepper. Bring to the boil, then turn the heat down and simmer gently for 30 minutes, stirring occasionally. Pass the sauce through a mouli-légumes or a sieve, if desired.

Tips
Tomato sauce should be cooked until it is pulpy and no longer watery. Depending on the amount of oil used in the recipe, the oil will either separate from the tomato base or give an oily

sheen to the surface of the sauce (both results are correct). It should pour easily off a spoon. If it is over-reduced, it will stick to the pasta instead of flowing over it. If insufficient oil is used, the sauce will be dull in colour and dense in consistency. It will also stick to the pasta.

Most homemade tomato sauces will keep for 3 days in the refrigerator and most can be frozen. If you want to prepare the sauce ahead, reheat it gently in a saucepan while the pasta cooks, or, if it has been frozen, thaw it in a microwave.

Pesto

The Ligurians claim that it's the balance of humidity and hot sun that gives the small leafed basil growing in the region its particularly sweet fragrance. It is turned into a creamy emulsion with pine nuts and olive oil and seasoned with garlic and parmesan, and a little fiore sardo or romano (pecorino cheeses). As such, it is seductive, tantalizingly aromatic, verdant and rich to eat. Like Bolognese sauce, many crimes have been committed in its name. Essentially, the Italians use it on pasta or a small dollop of it brings a touch of sunshine to a vegetable soup in winter. I also love it on bruschetta topped with tomatoes.

75g (3oz) fresh basil leaves
pinch of salt
2 cloves garlic, chopped
3 tbsp pine nuts
3 tbsp extra virgin olive oil
4 tbsp freshly grated parmesan cheese
2 tbsp freshly grated pecorino Romano cheese (if not available use 6 tbsp parmesan cheese)

MAKES 175ML (6FL OZ)

Make the pesto in a food processor. Put the basil leaves, salt, garlic, pine nuts and extra virgin olive oil in the processor bowl fitted with the steel chopping blade and process the mixture until blended. Transfer to a bowl, then mix in the cheeses by hand. Cover the surface with cling film and set aside until required. Pesto is most fragrant and verdant just after making, but it can be stored for up to a week. Put it in a small container and pour a film of oil over the top, then cover with a lid or plastic wrap and keep it refrigerated.

Focaccia

Commercially made focaccia is not always what it should be. If you like working with yeast, you'll find focaccia is easy enough to make, and you can flavour it according to your taste.

2 level tbsp dried yeast
100ml (3½fl oz) lukewarm water
450g (1lb) high-grade flour, plus about 50g
  (2oz) extra for kneading
2 tsp salt
250ml (8fl oz) of lukewarm water
50ml (2fl oz) olive oil for the dough, plus extra
  for brushing over the surface
salt mill

Stage 1

Put the yeast granules in a bowl and pour the first measure of lukewarm water over them. Leave for about 10 minutes or until dissolved and fluffy, then stir well. Sift the flour and 1 teaspoon of the salt into a large warmed bowl.

Make a well in the centre and pour in the dissolved yeast. Sprinkle flour over the yeast – just enough to cover it – then cover with a damp cloth and leave in a warm place for 20 minutes, or until the yeast breaks through the flour.

Stage 2

Blend in the second measure of lukewarm water, first using a fork, then your hands. Turn onto the work surface and knead for 8–10 minutes, using the extra flour to prevent sticking. (This can be done in a bread-mixing machine, in a food processor or with a food mixer fitted with a dough hook; follow the manufacturer's instructions.) Clean and dry the bowl, then smear it with a little oil. Put the ball of dough in the bowl, turn it over to coat it with oil, then cover with a damp cloth. Leave in a warm place for about 1–1½ hours, or until it has doubled in bulk.

Stage 3

Punch down the dough and turn it onto a floured work surface. Pat the dough flat, then sprinkle it with the remaining teaspoon of salt. Pour one-third of the olive oil into the centre, bundle up the dough, keeping the oil enclosed, then squash and squelch it until the oil is worked into the dough. Knead until smooth like putty. Repeat this step twice more, adding the rest of the oil (but no more salt), then finish off with 3–4 minutes of kneading.

Put the dough in an oiled bowl, turn it to coat all sides, cover with a damp cloth and leave in a warm place for 1–1½ hours or until it has doubled in bulk.

Stage 4

Punch down the dough, then turn it onto a well-used baking tray (scone tray) or a baking tray lined with a teflon baking sheet or baking parchment. Pat it down and spread into a large oval or rectangle nearly as big as the tray. Leave in a warm spot for 15–20 minutes to prove, or until it has slightly risen and feels puffy. Make dimples all over the surface with your fingertips, brush generously with oil and grind over a little salt.

Bake for 25–35 minutes in an oven preheated to 210°C/410°F/gas 6. Remove the tray from the oven halfway through cooking, brush the focaccia with oil, then return the tray to the oven, positioning it so that the side of the tray that was near the back of the oven is now near the oven door. Finish baking, remove from the oven and cool on a wire rack.

Flavourings
Sage or rosemary
Add 1 tablespoon of finely chopped fresh sage or rosemary along with the salt in Stage 3. Proceed as described. (Both these herbs are potent, so don't be tempted to add any more than the stated amount.)

Olives
If the olives are put on top of the focaccia, they will fall off (there's nothing worse than buying a loaf of olive bread which is devoid of olives!). Mixed into the dough, the olives give the focaccia a "shorter" texture and a fuller olive taste.

Use 100g (4oz/about 20) black olives, drained, and pat them dry with absorbent kitchen paper. Remove the stones with an olive pitter or cut them in half through the middle, twist apart and extract the stones. Chop the olives roughly.

Prepare the dough to the end of Stage 3. Punch it down and turn it onto a lightly floured surface. Scatter the olives and 1 teaspoon of dried marjoram or oregano (optional) over the dough. Knead briefly until well amalgamated. Proceed as for the basic focaccia dough.

Basic risotto

A bowl of well cooked risotto is a gloriously satisfying thing – grains of rice, plumped with tasty stock and flavourings, cooked until no longer chalky but still textural in the mouth, filling and nourishing – few dishes can beat it.

1.25L (2¼pt) chicken stock
2 tbsp olive oil
75g (3oz) butter
1 small onion, finely chopped
1 clove garlic, crushed
120ml (4fl oz) dry white wine
400g (14oz) Italian rice – arborio, vialone nano,
  carnaroli
¼ tsp salt
freshly ground black pepper to taste
freshly grated nutmeg
50g (2oz) freshly grated parmesan cheese, plus
  extra for serving

SERVES 4–6

Bring the chicken stock to simmering point, then set the heat so that it is kept very hot, but does not boil and evaporate.

Choose a 2.5–3 litre (4½–5 pint) heavy-based saucepan. Set it over a medium heat, put in the olive oil and half the butter and add the onion and garlic. Sauté until a pale golden colour, then pour in the wine and cook until it has nearly evaporated.

Tip in the unwashed rice, sauté for 2 minutes, stirring often with a wooden spoon, then stir in a ladleful of hot stock. This will evaporate quickly. Add a second ladleful of stock and stir, gently but continuously, until the stock has evaporated. Continue cooking in this way, stirring every few seconds (if you don't stir, the rice will stick to the pan), adding more stock once the rice is no longer sloppy. The rice is ready when, like pasta, the grains are al dente (still firm and only just cooked through, but no longer chalky inside). It requires a certain amount of judgment to arrive at the finishing point with the last ladleful of stock absorbed so that the rice is creamy, but not dry.

Remove the pan from the heat, add salt, black pepper, nutmeg, the rest of the butter and the cheese. Beat well for 1 minute, cover with a lid and leave for another minute to allow the flavours to fuse. Dish into hot plates and serve immediately.

Tips
Do not attempt these recipes with any rice other than the types suggested.

The rice should not be washed as the clinging starch provides creaminess.

Be aware that any defects in homemade stock will be emphasized through reduction. If you run out of stock, use water.

Be careful not to flood the rice with liquid because it will stew and not retain its structure.

Basic polenta

Polenta (ground maize) is a versatile, nutritionally rich ingredient that can easily form the cornerstone of a meal. To make half the quantity, simply halve the ingredients.

2.5L (4½pt) water
2 tsp salt
500g (1lb 2oz) polenta
large knob of butter
100g (4oz) freshly grated
  parmesan cheese

SERVES 10–12

Bring the water to the boil in a large, wide (not tall and narrow) saucepan. Add the salt, then sprinkle in the polenta a handful at a time, letting it fall through your fingers from a height. Stir continuously, using a wooden spoon. If you add the polenta too fast, it will form lumps (if this happens, fish them out because they will not break down during cooking). Once all the polenta is added, turn the heat to low and cook, giving three to four good stirs every 20 seconds or so, for 25 minutes.

When the polenta is cooked, it can be served immediately as a first course, like pasta. Beat in a large knob of butter and the freshly grated parmesan cheese. Serve with extra cheese and butter at the table.

Instant polenta
Regular polenta gives off a more pronounced corn aroma as it cooks and has a richer corn taste and grittier texture than instant polenta, but most people will find these differences hard to detect. If you're a purist, use regular polenta, which will take about 25 minutes to cook. But if you like speedy cooking, opt for the instant variety that will cook in about 5 minutes.

The wooden spoon test
The best way to check if slow-cooking polenta is done is to insert a wooden spoon in the centre of the pot. In the early stages of cooking, the spoon will flop to the sides. As the polenta cooks and firms, it will support the spoon. When it will stay upright in the middle of the polenta, it is cooked.

Rich shortcrust pastry

This is a useful pastry, which has an initially crisp, then melt-in-the-mouth texture and buttery taste. If you take the time to make it, you'll find it's superior in every way to commercially made pastry.

225g (8oz) plain flour
pinch of salt
175g (6oz) butter, softened
  until pliable
1 egg yolk
4–5 tbsp ice-cold water (chill
  the water in the freezer)

Sift the flour and salt into a large mixing bowl. Cut the butter into large lumps and drop it into the flour. Using two knives, cut the butter through the flour until the pieces of butter are like small marbles. Use your fingertips to rub the butter into the flour until the mixture resembles coarse breadcrumbs.

Mix the egg yolk and 3 tablespoons of water together and add it all at once to the flour mixture; if the pastry seems a little dry and flaky during mixing, sprinkle the extra tablespoon of water, or part of it, on the dry flakes. Stir with a knife to combine. Lightly knead with your hands and turn out onto a cool, dry, lightly floured surface. Knead briefly until it is smooth. Wrap in plastic food wrap and refrigerate for 30 minutes.

Roll out thinly with a lightly floured rolling pin and line the flan ring. Cut off any excess pastry, fold it up and re-roll. Cut out small tartlet bases or line into a small dish and freeze for later use.

Pastry made in the food processor
Put the flour, salt and cubed butter in the bowl of a food processor fitted with the metal chopping blade. Process until the mixture resembles breadcrumbs. Mix the egg yolk and water and pour it over the flour and butter mixture. Pulse until the mixture forms clumps. Turn it out onto a dry work surface and knead lightly, with a little flour if necessary, until it is smooth. Wrap in plastic food wrap and chill for 45 minutes.

Crisp pastry
A flan ring placed on a baking tray produces a crisper base to the pastry, as any moisture can freely run out from underneath the flan ring and evaporate. In a flan dish the moisture is trapped and can cause the pastry to become soggy.

Quantities

A 20cm (7¾in) flan ring or dish requires rich shortcrust pastry made with 170g (6oz) plain flour, but I always make a standard 225g (8oz) batch of pastry, because the ingredients are easier to work with (ever tried splitting an egg?). Any leftover pastry can be used to line a smaller flan ring, tartlet tins or a small pie dish. It is no more difficult to make a double batch of pastry (450g/1lb plain flour). This makes enough pastry to line three 20cm (7¾in) flan rings.

If you want to freeze the pastry, it is more convenient to do this after lining the flan ring or tins. Once frozen, the pastry shape/s can be slipped out of the rings or tins (freeing them for other uses) and stored in a sealed plastic freezer bag for 6 months. This allows you to collect tartlet bases until you have enough for a recipe and, if you have made a double batch of pastry, you will have extra flan bases on hand when you want to put a quick meal together. Thaw the pastry cases for 5 minutes at room temperature, then slip them back into their rings or tins. Cook once thawed, but while the pastry is still chilled.

Baking blind

To bake blind, the pastry is first lined with paper, then filled with baking beans and baked. Paper is used to make the removal of the beans easier and to prevent the beans becoming embedded in the pastry. I use tissue paper rather than grease-proof paper – greaseproof paper becomes dry and brittle and the sharp creases in the paper can cut the pastry when you remove it from the flan. Tissue paper, if well crinkled, moulds easily into any shape, is soft after baking and can be lifted out without disturbing the pastry. Baking beans are used to support the pastry until it is cooked or set in position. (Don't waste money on expensive metal pellets, as you can use inexpensive ingredients such as small pasta shapes, rice or dried beans, and replace them periodically.)

Partially baking blind

This produces crisper pastry (particularly useful when the filling is very moist or if your oven does not have good bottom heat – the most common cause of soggy pastry). This method is also used when the filling is quick-cooking (in other words, it would cook before the pastry).

Fully baking blind

This method is used when the pastry case is to be filled with a cooked filling or a combination of a cooked filling and raw ingredients (such as custard and fresh fruit).

For recipes in this book, bake pastry blind for 10–15 minutes in an oven preheated to 180°C/350°F/gas 4 or until the pastry rim is set in position.

Pizza dough

In a domestic oven it's hard to recreate a typical Neapolitan pizza with its puffed, thin, crisp crust, mottled with lightly charred spots and tasting faintly of smoke. But invest in a pizza stone and you'll come very close to the real thing, and certainly make pizzas that will leave most commercially prepared products for dead.

1 tsp dried yeast and 120ml (4fl oz) warm water
1 tbsp olive oil
225g (8oz) high-grade flour or bread flour
1 tsp salt
2 tsp gluten (if using bread flour, omit the gluten)
coarse cornmeal

Put the dried yeast in a small bowl and pour in the warm water. Stir once, then leave for 10 minutes until dissolved. Mix in the oil, stirring well. Sieve the flour, salt and gluten into a bowl. Make a well in the centre and pour in the yeast mixture.

Mix together with a large fork, then knead together with your fingers. Turn the dough onto a work surface and knead until smooth. Knead for 8–10 minutes, using a little extra flour to prevent sticking if necessary. Alternatively, knead the dough in an electric food mixer for several minutes with a dough hook, according to the manufacturer's instructions. Put the ball of dough into an oiled bowl, turn it over to coat it in oil, then cover with a damp cloth. Leave in a warm place for 1–1½ hours, or until it has doubled in bulk.

Turn the dough onto a baking sheet sprinkled with coarse cornmeal. Press or roll it into a round circle approximately 32cm (12½in) in diameter. Rest the dough uncovered for 5 minutes (or wrap and refrigerate it for up to 12 hours, bringing it back to room temperature before continuing), then assemble the topping as per the chosen recipe.

Meanwhile, heat the pizza stone for about 45 minutes on the bottom shelf of an oven preheated to 250°C/480°F/gas 9 then lower to 225°C/430°F/gas 7. Using thick oven gloves, remove the hot stone from the oven to the stove top. Quickly slide the pizza onto the stone, then return it to the oven. Alternatively, use a pizza paddle. Cook the pizza for about 10 minutes or until it is golden and bubbling on top and browned on the edges. Transfer the pizza to a large plate and serve. If you don't have a pizza cutter (a sharp wheel), use kitchen scissors to snip the pizza into wedges.

Glossary

Al dente Italian cooking term, literally meaning "to the tooth". It describes pasta which is cooked, but still firm to the bite.

Anchovies Look for plump anchovies sold in glass jars. Don't fry anchovies in hot oil as they seize and harden and can become bitter. Cook them gently, stirring, until they dissolve into a paste.

Antipasto Italian word used to describe a group of foods served as hors d'oeuvres (plural is antipasti), literally meaning, "before the meal".

Balsamic vinegar This superior vinegar, a speciality of Modena, is made using a centuries-old technique. The juice of trebbiano grapes is boiled down to a syrup, then poured into wooden barrels. It is left for at least five years, in some cases longer. The resulting vinegar is aromatic, spicy and sweet-sour to taste. It should be used sparingly. Most of the cheap balsamic vinegars are based on caramel, not grape syrup.

Bird's-eye chillies Small, dried hot chilli peppers, the best substitute for the small hot chilli used in Italy.

Bruschetta Toasted bread doused with extra virgin olive oil (use ciabatta or thick crusted textural bread).

Capers Capers packed in salt have a truer caper flavour than those packed in vinegar or brine. The salt should be white, not yellowing (which is an indication of age). Wash off loose salt before using and soak the capers in several changes of warm water until they lose any excessive salty taste.

Ciabatta Slipper-shaped loaf of bread with a holey texture and a thin, chewy crust.

Emilian egg pasta This pasta is a treat. Made from pasta dough enriched with eggs, it is much more yellow than regular Italian dried pasta. Maltagliati are odd-shaped pieces, scraps if you like (the word means "badly cut"), the off-cuts from making stuffed pasta. In Italy it is available either fresh or dried.

Frittata Italian egg dish, like a flattish omelette.

Herbs Herbs are used both fresh and dried in Italian cooking. Italian parsley has flat unfurled leaves with a fresh, grassy, just-picked taste and is always used fresh, as is basil and occasionally mint. Rosemary, bay, sage, oregano, thyme and marjoram are used fresh or dried.

Mascarpone A very rich, mild-tasting creamy "cheese" used in desserts and savoury dishes.

Mouli-légumes Also known as a mouli, this inexpensive and almost indestructible piece of equipment is the best way to purée fresh tomatoes (because it catches the seeds, cores and skins) and potatoes (it aerates the potato, making it light, fluffy and lump-free). A food processor doesn't do either of these jobs well because it crushes the tomato seeds, making the sauce bitter and makes a potato purée gluey.

Mozzarella Traditionally this cheese was made from buffalo's milk, but it is now usually made from cow's milk. Sold as a fresh cheese, but also available vacuum-packed in whey. Bocconcini are small bite-sized balls of mozzarella.

Olives I recommend using firm Italian or Greek black olives in the recipes in this book as they have good flavour and colour, and do not cook down to a mush that can darken sauces. Add them towards the end of cooking. When green olives are called for, choose large, plump green ones.

Panettone A dome-shaped cake, with a light texture and buttery taste, studded with peel and raisins. Popular around Christmas-time.

Parmesan cheese (parmigiano-Reggiano)
Has an intoxicating aroma and a spicy flavour with an interesting granular texture. Parmesan look-alikes tend to be highly seasoned, soapy, dry, coarse-textured or inferior in some way. They have no place in authentic Italian cuisine. Parmigiano-Reggiano melts without running, browns well, isn't greasy and doesn't become rubbery. It is quickly digested (even by infants) and low in calories. Buy it in the piece and treble-wrap it in aluminium foil. Keep it in the door or the coolest part of the fridge. If storing for a long period, change the foil every so often and wipe the rind clean. It can be frozen for a short period, but it will start to dry out after a month. Grate parmesan as required, because it quickly loses its aroma and flavour.

Pecorino This is the name given to Italian cheeses made from ewe's milk. The second name indicates where the cheese is from, or the style in which it is made, i.e. pecorino Romano, pecorino Sardo, pecorino Siciliano etc.

Pesto A rich, green, oily sauce, made with basil, garlic, pine nuts, olive oil and parmesan and Romano cheeses. The best comes from Genova, they say, as the sea air gives the basil a particular character.

Pine nuts Seeds of the stone pine, pine nuts are small and creamy-coloured with a nutty, creamy taste. Buy in small quantities as they quickly turn rancid.

Pizza paddle A flat wooden paddle with a long handle used to move pizzas in and out of a pizza oven.

Pizza stone A heavy ceramic plate which emulates the high heat of a pizza or bread oven. The pizza stone is heated in the oven until very hot. When the pizza is put on the stone it is given a blast of bottom heat which helps the dough puff and blister and cook quickly.

Polenta It's usually a rich golden colour, but in the Veneto region they are rather proud of another variety, white in colour with a less strong corn flavour and a very smooth texture. Today polenta is usually ground from corn, but there is a polenta made from buckwheat, a speciality of Treviso. It is often sold preboiled, in a slab, ready to fry, grill or bake.

Porcini mushrooms Earthy, woodsy-smelling richly flavoured mushrooms (*Boletus edulis*), available fresh in Europe in autumn and spring, and driedall year round. Drying them intensifies their aroma and taste. Sold in small cellophane bags, make sure you choose a bag with large, pale pieces of porcini, not one full of crumbs and dust. Stored airtight, they last for months.

Poussin A baby chicken.

Prosciutto This famous ham (sometimes referred to as Parma ham) is sold either as *prosciutto crudo*, a raw ham cured by air and salt (not, as is often presumed, by smoking) or *prosciutto cotto*, a cooked version. In this book, prosciutto refers to the raw, cured ham. Prosciutto crudo is sweet and delicate with creamy, sweet-tasting fat. It is sliced very thin and eaten as an antipasto component or used in pasta sauces and stuffings. Substitute thinly sliced ham off the bone if you have to.

Radicchio *Rosso di Verona* or *rosa di Chioggia* looks like a small red cabbage. Used raw in salads it has a pleasantly bitter taste that works well with strongly flavoured dressings made with garlic, capers and mustard. "Radicchio di Treviso" has long tapering leaves, is less bitter and is best doused in olive oil and grilled, or used in risottos and sauces.

Ricotta cheese A soft curd, low-fat cheese made from whey, ricotta is a by-product of cheesemaking. Used in savoury and sweet dishes.

Risotto rice These varieties of rice have short, stubby grains and have the ability to absorb plenty of flavoursome liquid while giving out a creamy starch, yet still maintain a firm al dente structure. Arborio rice, probably the best known and most freely available variety, makes a sticky risotto, but each grain can still be separated from the mass. Vialone nano is particularly good for Venetian-style risottos where the desired result is a little more liquid than risottos from other regions. Perhaps the best, but hardest to find and the most expensive, is carnaroli rice, which produces a rich creamy risotto while maintaining a firm texture.

Roma or plum tomatoes Egg-shaped tomatoes with plenty of flesh and few seeds, which makes them ideal for sauce-making.

Salt The most indispensable ingredient in the Italian kitchen, when used correctly, is the cook's best friend. It draws out those nuances of flavour which may never have been brought to the fore. Salt sprinkled on cooked food is not the same; you are likely to taste only salt. Use coarse rock salt for cooking pasta (it's generally cheaper) and sea salt for other uses.

Scaloppine This is the Italian name for the thin slices of veal cut from a single muscle off the top of the animal's leg. In France, the same cut is known as an escalope. In English the names scallop and schnitzel are used, but not scallopini, which is the name for small star-shaped squash.

Stock Italian stock (*brodo*) is much lighter than French stock. It is usually made from veal bones or chicken carcasses, or both, and vegetables. Use vegetable cooking water or diluted chicken stock as a substitute.

Vin Santo This sweet, or semi-dry, wine is made from grapes left to dry until they turn raisiny. The wine is then transferred to small barrels and left to age for at least 2 years. It is often served with hard biscuits, called *cantucci*, which are dipped into the Vin Santo to soften them.

Index